"Conversion is essential and misunderstood. Lawrence understands this and explains what the Bible teaches simply and compellingly. This small book is a big gift."

> **Mark Dever,** pastor, Capitol Hill Baptist Church, Washington, DC; president, 9Marks

"This discipleship resource has it all—pastoral clarity, urgent relevance, practical brevity, and faithfulness to the Scriptures. Line by line, every chapter contains fodder for significant discussions on what the Word says about evangelism, conversion, and the church. I'm so thankful that Michael Lawrence wrote this book—I'll be referring to it often."

> **Gloria Furman**, author, *The Pastor's Wife*; *Missional Motherhood*; and *Alive in Him*

"Down-to-earth, clear, practical, straight shooting, biblically cogent treatment of the nature and necessity of conversion. This is an excellent book."

> **David F. Wells,** distinguished senior research professor, Gordon-Conwell Theological Seminary; author, *The Courage to Be Protestant: Truth-Lovers, Marketers, and Emergents in the Postmodern World*

"This is a biblically informed and extremely relevant book for pastors and sheep alike. Michael Lawrence hits the nail on the head when it comes to the conversion experience. Being born again is not the result of a superficial, emotional, and man-motivated prayer. This is a call to reexamine the Scriptures to see that conversion is a divine work from beginning to end, which should be externally evident by the way true disciples live in love-motivated obedience to Christ; by the interest they show in belonging to a local body of believers to whom they are accountable; and by the way they live the gospel in holiness and practice evangelism. Conversion requires repentance, and repentance requires a work of the Holy Spirit. I am delighted to see this book published at this time."

Miguel Núñez, senior pastor, International Baptist Church, Santo Domingo, Dominican Republic; president, Wisdom & Integrity Ministries

"In this important book Michael Lawrence outlines the biblical theology of conversion with clarity. The aim here is not to suggest that conversion makes people nice, because it is possible to be nice and not be converted. On the other hand, conversion is not a matter of mere subjectivity, for it is possible to feel converted and not be. Lawrence argues that conversion is an act that begins with God (regeneration) and bears fruit in men (repentance and faith). This overflow of God's grace not only allows us to repent and believe, but also enables us to be inserted into the people that God created in Christ Jesus. In short, conversion culminates in membership in the local church. I heartily recommend this book."

Jonas Madureira, senior pastor, Reformed Baptist Church, São Paulo, Brazil

"Real conversion is not a facade of 'niceness,' nor does it depend on a decision made once years ago. True conversion is nothing less than rebirth, new creation, and new life in Christ. This book offers a clear and compelling account of conversion, according to the Scriptures. And it shows how essential a right understanding is for the life of every believer and every church. Highly recommended."

Constantine R. Campbell, associate professor of New Testament, Trinity Evangelical Divinity School

"With theological precision, but with plain and accessible language, Michael Lawrence guides us through the Scriptures to help us understand what true conversion is and what are the fruits that evidence it. This is a book I would like to place in the hands of all members of our church."

Sugel Michelen, pastor, Iglesia Bíblica del Señor Jesucristo, Santo Domingo, Dominican Republic

"If there is a subject that Satan has tried to confuse people about, it is the nature of true conversion. What better way to get religious people to land in hell than by letting them think they are converted when in fact they are not? Michael Lawrence has clarified this matter for us by building up from the oft-forgotten truth of regeneration, which is the foundation of conversion. He ends with the practical implications of this truth when held in biblical proportions. His pen is that of a skillful writer, and it oozes with wise pastoral counsel. I highly recommend that those of us who know that we are truly converted should also read this delightful book so as to avoid leading others astray."

Conrad Mbewe, pastor, Kabwata Baptist Church, Lusaka, Zambia; chancellor, African Christian University, Lusaka, Zambia

9Marks: Building Healthy Churches

Edited by Mark Dever and Jonathan Leeman

Deacons: How They Serve and Strengthen the Church, Matt Smethurst (2021)

Corporate Worship: How the Church Gathers as God's People, Matt Merker (2021)

Prayer: How Praying Together Shapes the Church, John Onwuchekwa (2018)

Biblical Theology: How the Church Faithfully Teaches the Gospel, Nick Roark and Robert Cline (2018)

Missions: How the Local Church Goes Global, Andy Johnson (2017)

Conversion: How God Creates a People, Michael Lawrence (2017)

Discipling: How to Help Others Follow Jesus, Mark Dever (2016)

The Gospel: How the Church Portrays the Beauty of Christ, Ray Ortlund (2014)

Expositional Preaching: How We Speak God's Word Today, David R. Helm (2014)

Evangelism: How the Whole Church Speaks of Jesus, J. Mack Stiles (2014)

Church Elders: How to Shepherd God's People Like Jesus, Jeramie Rinne (2014)

Sound Doctrine: How a Church Grows in the Love and Holiness of God, Bobby Jamieson (2013)

Church Membership: How the World Knows Who Represents Jesus, Jonathan Leeman (2012)

Church Discipline: How the Church Protects the Name of Jesus, Jonathan Leeman (2012)

BUILDING HEALTHY CHURCHES

CONVERSION

HOW GOD
CREATES
A PEOPLE

MICHAEL LAWRENCE

CROSSWAY®

WHEATON, ILLINOIS

Hardcover ISBN: 978-1-4335-5649-4
ePub ISBN: 978-1-4335-5652-4
PDF ISBN: 978-1-4335-5650-0
Mobipocket ISBN: 978-1-4335-5651-7

Library of Congress Cataloging-in-Publication Data
Names: Lawrence, Michael, 1966– author.
Title: Conversion : how God creates a people / Michael Lawrence.
Description: Wheaton : Crossway, 2017. | Series: 9Marks: building healthy churches | Includes bibliographical references and index.
Identifiers: LCCN 2016054948 (print) | LCCN 2017017632 (ebook) | ISBN 9781433556500 (pdf) | ISBN 9781433556517 (mobi) | ISBN 9781433556524 (epub) | ISBN 9781433556494 (hc)
Subjects: LCSH: Conversion—Christianity. | Discipling (Christianity) | Church.
Classification: LCC BT780 (ebook) | LCC BT780 .L39 2017 (print) | DDC 248.2/4—dc23
LC record available at https://lccn.loc.gov/2016054948

Crossway is a publishing ministry of Good News Publishers.

LB		31	30	29	28	27	26	25	24	23	22
17	16	15	14	13	12	11	10	9	8	7	6	5

For Adrienne,
whose love for me
reminds me of the gospel
every day

"Once you were not a people,
but now you are God's people;
once you had not received mercy,
but now you have received mercy."
(1 Pet. 2:10)

CONTENTS

SERIES PREFACE

The 9Marks series of books is premised on two basic ideas. First, the local church is far more important to the Christian life than many Christians today perhaps realize.

Second, local churches grow in life and vitality as they organize their lives around God's Word. God speaks. Churches should listen and follow. It's that simple. When a church listens and follows, it begins to look like the One it is following. It reflects his love and holiness. It displays his glory. A church will look like him as it listens to him.

So our basic message to churches is, don't look to the best business practices or the latest styles; look to God. Start by listening to God's Word again.

Out of this overall project comes the 9Marks series of books. Some target pastors. Some target church members. Hopefully all will combine careful biblical examination, theological reflection, cultural consideration, corporate application, and even a bit of individual exhortation. The best Christian books are always both theological and practical.

It's our prayer that God will use this volume and the others to help prepare his bride, the church, with radiance and splendor for the day of his coming.

INTRODUCTION

Recently I was talking to one of my friends about his two adult kids. He's worried about them. They're not into drugs or partying. They both have healthy, warm relationships with their parents and peers. They went to excellent universities and excelled. They're athletic, ambitious, beautiful, charming young adults. If they were your kids, you'd be proud of them, as my friend is. Still, you'd be worried, because neither of them seems to have the slightest interest in Jesus Christ. And to make matters more difficult, both of them identify themselves as Christians.

These two kids were raised in the church. They learned their Bible lessons in Sunday school. They were active in the youth group. They were never outwardly rebellious. They each prayed "the sinner's prayer." They were baptized. When they went off to college, they kept the nice, moral behavior they'd learned at church, but . . .

They basically left Jesus behind. They didn't abandon the name of "Christian." They simply stopped showing interest in the Christian life.

You understand why my friend is worried. He has nice kids who are convinced they don't need Jesus because they already have him. Yet the more he watches their adult lives unfold, the less and less confident he is that they even know Jesus at all.

I serve in a church where I've had a conversation like this with scores of parents. It's a heartbreaking conversation, not least because these parents feel betrayed: they did what they were told to do! They raised their children right. They led them in the sinner's prayer. They took them to church and enrolled them in all the right programs—all in the confident expectation that by doing so, their children would love Jesus too.

And it didn't work.

At this point, you might expect me to launch into a chapter or book on parenting. But I'll leave that to more seasoned and experienced hands. And it's not clear to me anyway that the problem here is a problem of parenting. Many great, conscientious parents in our churches are in the same predicament as my friend.

Instead, I suggest we focus on two other problems. First, there is a problem of theology—specifically, our theology of conversion. Second, there is a problem with how we apply that theology to our church. How do we work out our beliefs in practical ways that express those truths we claim to believe?

Too often our confessional theology says one thing, while our practical theology says something else. We say that regeneration makes us new creatures in Christ, but then we teach our kids a moralism that atheists could duplicate.

We say that Christianity is about a trusting relationship with Jesus, but then we treat it like checking a box on a decision card.

We say that only the Holy Spirit transfers a person from the kingdom of darkness to the kingdom of light, but then we employ the marketing tools used for getting someone to switch brands of toothpaste.

Again and again, what we claim in our doctrinal statements about conversion doesn't match what our churches practice or their ministry models. So it shouldn't surprise us that our kids end up being something less than Christian.

Of course, this isn't a problem that just affects parents and children. It affects churches. When our converts from one evangelistic campaign are nowhere to be seen when the next campaign rolls around; when our members treat church as optional, to be balanced with sports leagues and vacation houses; when giving and attendance fall far short of the membership numbers; when volunteers are hard to find unless it's a social event, the problem probably isn't our evangelism technique, or poor leadership, or uninteresting worship services, or bad volunteer management. The problem may well be our practical theology of conversion. Too often we treat the symptoms. But what we really need is to go after the underlying disease.

And that's what this book aims to do.

In the chapters that follow, I want to think carefully about the doctrine of conversion from the Scriptures. But I don't want to stop there. I want to think about the difference doctrine should make in the life of the church—from the way we go about evangelism, to our membership and discipleship practices, to how we think about the church as a whole.

In other words, this is a book of doctrine, and this is a book of practice. It is a book about conversion, and it is a book about the church. After all, God creates a people through conversion. Show me someone's doctrine of conversion, and I can tell you a lot about his church. Or rather: show me his church, and I will describe his *functional* doctrine of conversion, regardless of what he might say in pen and ink. Our churches embody our doctrine.

So getting our theology of conversion right means more than having correct theology. It means developing ministry practices that both reflect and undergird our theological convictions.

Good theology is intensely practical, and if it's not, then it isn't worth the name.

1

NEW, NOT NICE

The Necessity of Regeneration

In the introduction, I mentioned my friend who was concerned that his well-mannered adult children weren't really Christians. You might say they were *nice*, but not *new*—not new creations.

His experience raises questions about the doctrine of conversion, as well as what that doctrine should look like in the life of a church. It's crucial to get both our doctrine and our practices right. Churches should believe that God makes people radically new, not just nice. But not only should they be able to write this out on paper, but they should also live it out. What does that look like?

In two of the most important passages in Scripture for understanding conversion, both the prophet Ezekiel and Jesus help us answer that question. Let's start with Jesus. He said we must be "born again" to enter the kingdom of God. Speaking to a Pharisee named Nicodemus, Jesus observed,

> "Unless one is born again he cannot see the kingdom of God."
> Nicodemus said to him, "How can a man be born when he is

old? Can he enter a second time into his mother's womb and be born?" Jesus answered, "Truly, truly, I say to you, unless one is born of water and the Spirit, he cannot enter the kingdom of God. That which is born of the flesh is flesh, and that which is born of the Spirit is spirit. Do not marvel that I said to you, 'You must be born again.' The wind blows where it wishes, and you hear its sound, but you do not know where it comes from or where it goes. So it is with everyone who is born of the Spirit." (John 3:3–8)

THE APPEAL OF NICE

It's worth recognizing the powerful appeal of nice.

Nicodemus and Pharisees like him believed that people entered the kingdom of God by being nice, which for them meant being a good Jew: keeping the Law of Moses, going to the temple, offering all the right sacrifices, and staying away from Gentiles. I'm not suggesting Nicodemus thought he was perfect. He probably knew he should be a better person. Perhaps that's why he went to Jesus in the first place. But at the end of the day, moral righteousness was the standard to which he aspired. Nice people got into the kingdom.

These days, there are lots of different kinds of nice. There's the polite but detached tolerance of "live and let live" nice. There's the socially conscious and politically engaged nice. There's religious nice in many different denominational and faith-community forms. There's "spiritual but not religious" nice. There's even what's known in my town as "Portland nice," a sort of nonconfrontational, "let's not make you feel uncomfortable, even though we're silently judging and dismissing you in our minds" nice.

But for all the different kinds of nice, the appeal of nice hasn't changed much in the last two thousand years. To be a nice person, a good person, a person who's becoming a better person, is to feel good about yourself. It's that appeal of moral self-commendation that binds our modern variations together into a common religious program that Nicodemus would have recognized (see Luke 10:25–29). Nice allows you to commend yourself to others, and maybe even to God. Nice gives you the means of self-justification and the ability to vindicate your life to whoever is asking. That's appealing.

THE ASSUMPTIONS OF NICE

The appeal of nice is always based on three ideas: an optimistic view of human beings, a domesticated view of God, and a view of religion as a means of moral self-reform. Fundamentally, Nicodemus assumes that he is *able* to do whatever he needs to do in order to vindicate himself to God. He assumes that *God* is the kind of God that will be pleased with his best efforts, and he assumes that the point of *religion* is to help him become a better person. This is how nice works. God wants me to be good. I'm able to be good. Religion will help.

No churches ever explicitly teach the religion of nice. In fact, they typically teach the exact opposite. But those same churches are filled with people who believe that God will accept them based on how good they've been. I've heard it on too many living room couches and nursing home beds. Not perfect—no one ever says that—but good enough.

Can you relate to Nicodemus? I can. When I was a young college student, I began to worry that God wouldn't accept me.

So I started a little conversation with God: "God, I will quit drinking. God, I'll start reading my Bible and going to church more often. So please don't send me to hell, but let me into heaven." Nicodemus and I had the same assumptions. I can be good. God will be impressed. Religion will help. This wasn't the prayer of a pagan. It was the prayer of someone who'd grown up in the church, who'd heard the gospel countless times, and who believed he was a Christian. Yet the religion of nice corresponded to what my heart—like every fallen heart—desired. I wanted to be able to justify myself. And nice was the way to do it.

The role of religion in the project of self-justification is well encapsulated by a project run by World Weavers in support of the Blood Foundation, a nongovernment organization in Thailand. The program immerses people in different faith traditions for a month for a small fee. They offer "[Buddhist] Monk for a Month," "Muslim for a Month," and "the Rasta Roots Spiritual Experience."[1] The assumption is there's no need to convert or become a true believer. Rather, religions help people become better, nicer people, and any religion can do the trick.

This assumption that all religions are essentially the same underneath their cultural wrappers is why so many people in the West have abandoned religion altogether. If the point is simply to be a better person today than I was yesterday, then why do I need any religion at all? Of course, the real question that must be answered is, by whose standards will my self-justification project be measured? My own? Society's? Which society's? God's? If religion is nothing more than an aid to self-improvement, we'd all be emotionally better off if we abandoned the moral and religious project of self-justification and instead adopted the psychological project of personal growth and self-acceptance. The therapeutic professions have been telling us this for the last century.

My point is this: the appeal of nice is not only that it panders to our prideful desire to justify ourselves, it also dispenses with the need to justify ourselves to God altogether. It substitutes feeling good about myself for being in right relationship with God and neighbor. It numbs my sense of guilt, soothes my anxious insecurity, and promotes the illusion that I am in control of my own fate on judgment day.

THE PRACTICE OF NICE

What makes the moralistic program of nice difficult to spot in our evangelical churches is that it's almost never taught explicitly. Instead, it's the natural condition of our unregenerate selves. It follows us into the church like walking inside with the aroma of the outdoors: it's hard to smell on yourself because you are so accustomed to it. But the smell shows up in a number of ways:

- We condemn the world's sin more than our own.
- We put sins in a hierarchy, and tolerate some sins (especially our own) more than others.
- In church, we sing songs and pray prayers of praise, not songs and prayers of confession.
- We describe our own sins as "mistakes."
- We use Bible stories to teach children to be good rather than to point them to a Savior: "Be like David" not "You need a new and better David, who is Christ."

21

Perhaps the main way we teach nice is how we present Christ. We commend Christ and the gospel as a method of self-improvement. It's not that we fail to talk about the cross or even sin. It's that sin is presented as a problem primarily for how it messes up our lives and relationships and gets in the way of our goals. And Jesus Christ is presented as the one who will change all that. We tell people that Jesus will make a difference in their marriages and in their parenting. Jesus will bring love, joy, and peace to their home. Jesus will give them renewed purpose at work. Come to Jesus, and he will make a difference in your life.

Jesus, of course, does make a difference in the lives of believers. It's just not the difference of a better life now in all the ways we might want. After all, what did Jesus say? "If anyone would come after me, let him deny himself and take up his cross and follow me" (Matt. 16:24). That means Jesus might make a difference in your marriage by giving you the grace to persevere with a spouse who no longer loves you. He might bring love, joy, and peace to your home by making you an agent rather than a recipient of those things. He might give you renewed purpose at work by changing your attitude rather than your job description.

When we present Jesus as the solution to our self-diagnosed problems, many on the outside of the church aren't convinced. They don't stop playing the game of nice. They just don't see the need to play the game *at church* or evidence that we play it better than they do.

Meanwhile, people inside the church are confused as to what biblical Christianity is in the first place. So many of us learned the message of nice in churches that introduced us to a Jesus who promised to improve us, not a Jesus who calls his followers to die to themselves; these churches taught us to be nice without making sure we were new. I fear this is why so many of my friends' children have walked away from Christianity. They haven't given up on nice. They've simply discovered that they don't need Jesus to be nice.

THE NECESSITY OF NEW

The appeal of nice is strong. It plays to our vanity and pride. But three times in John 3 Jesus confronts us with the need to be made new:

- "Unless one is born again he cannot see the kingdom of God." (v. 3)
- "Unless one is born of water and the Spirit, he cannot enter the kingdom of God." (v. 5)
- "You must be born again." (v. 7)

If we would be right with God, we don't need to improve ourselves. We need a complete restart. In fact, the Bible uses several theological concepts to describe what Jesus means:

- *Regeneration*, which means being born again, with an emphasis on the divine source of that new life (1 Pet. 1:3)
- *Re-creation*, which means being made anew as part of the end-time new creation (2 Cor. 5:17; Gal. 6:15)
- *Transformation*, which means being given a new nature (Col. 3:10)

A radical change must occur in us. But the word that the Bible never uses to describe what Jesus is talking about is *reformation*.

You might reform a church, but not a dead heart. The personal change that Jesus says we need goes much deeper; it reaches down to our very nature.

According to Scripture, God made us to worship him, to love him, and to find in him our deepest satisfaction. That was our nature as he originally created it. But when our first parents decided to rebel against God, they didn't just break a rule; they corrupted their nature. Theologians call this "original sin," and we have all inherited it. Created with a nature to love God, we now have a nature that is bent on loving self. From birth, Paul says, we are dead in our sins, and walk in the passions of our flesh (Eph. 2:1–3). We're like dead men walking. This is why nice doesn't work. We must be made new.

THE PROBLEM OF NICE AND THE PROMISE OF NEW

The necessity of being born again flows from five biblical truths: the inability of human beings, the holiness of God, the grace of the gospel, the power of God's Spirit, and the creation of a people.

1. *Our inability.* Jesus makes a radical distinction between flesh and Spirit, that is, between us and God: "That which is born of the flesh is flesh, and that which is born of the Spirit is spirit" (John 3:6). No matter how good the flesh is, it cannot produce the spiritual life that's needed if we would be right with God (see also Rom. 8:5–8). It's not that we tried hard, but fell short. Or meant well, but got sidetracked. It's that our sinful nature desires to please the flesh rather than God. Even when we do the right thing morally, we do it for the wrong reasons—to justify ourselves and bring ourselves glory. This

is one reason the Bible describes us as dead and not just sick (Eph. 2:1–3). Like a dead person, we are incapable of loving God for God's sake.

2. *God's holiness.* What's more, God is not like us. The Bible is unrelenting in its presentation of God's holiness. God's holiness means that he's in a different category from us altogether. He's utterly set apart from sin and consecrated to his own glory. He's uncompromising in his goodness. He refuses to tolerate evil. He's not impressed with how good we are—with our nice—because we pursue niceness for our own glory rather than God's (see Isa. 64:6). So we stand under God's judgment, another reason the Bible refers to us as *dead*. And it's a judgment we deserve.

3. *God's grace.* Yet there's good news: God is gracious! God himself took the initiative toward us. While we were still his enemies, God sent his Son to take on our flesh and to live the life we were originally created to live. He lived not a nice life, not a good life, but a perfect and sinless life, a life wholly devoted to God's glory. Then Jesus offered his life on the cross as a sacrifice, taking God's wrath on himself as a substitute for anyone who would turn from his sins and put his faith in him. To prove God accepted his sacrifice, three days later Jesus rose from the dead.

4. *God's Spirit.* But that's just the beginning of God's initiative toward us. Jesus speaks about the Spirit's work in John 3, which he compares to the wind over which we have no control. When God regenerates us, the Holy Spirit of God instantaneously unites us to Christ. In that union the Spirit takes all the benefit of what the Son has done—his resurrection life, his

righteousness, his grace—and applies it all to us. This changes our nature, gives us the new birth, makes us new creatures. We then turn to Christ in repentance and faith, are justified by his grace, and are adopted into his family to follow him in a relationship of love and trust.

5. *Creation of a people.* Hundreds of years before Jesus's conversation with Nicodemus, God promised his grace and Spirit through the prophet Ezekiel. He also promised that he would make us a people.

> And I will give you a new heart, and a new spirit I will put within you. And I will remove the heart of stone from your flesh and give you a heart of flesh. And I will put my Spirit within you, and cause you to walk in my statutes and be careful to obey my rules . . . and you shall be my people, and I will be your God. And I will deliver you from all your uncleannesses. (Ezek. 36:26–29)

God has kept this promise through the work of Christ. He makes us new creatures. He grants us his Spirit. He makes us a people. And he forgives our sin.

WHY THE DOCTRINE OF REGENERATION MATTERS FOR THE CHRISTIAN

The truth that God actually makes us new has enormous implications for the life of the church, both corporately and individually.

Let's start with the individual. A Christian has a new nature, one that is bent toward God rather than away from him. Jonathan Edwards described the regenerate person as someone who has been given a taste for God, like someone who has tasted honey and now has a sense of its sweetness. That doesn't mean that a Christian doesn't sin anymore. But the old nature is no longer in control. Christ is, and the new nature has a new set of desires for God. The new creation may just be a seed, but that seed will grow.

What does that mean for my friend's children, whom I introduced in the introduction? To begin with, it means they needed to be taught that a Christian isn't someone who prays a prayer and tries hard to be good. Instead, a Christian is someone whose heart has been transformed by God's grace, who is characterized by repentance and faith, who desires to be with God and know him more. It means churches should not offer assurance through baptism so quickly, but encourage children to examine themselves to see if they're in the faith (2 Cor. 13:5); to look for fruit that the Spirit produces (Gal. 5:22–23); to follow Jesus in self-sacrificing love rather than self-righteous morality (1 John 4:7); to pursue a relationship of love with God through loving brothers and sisters in Christ (1 John 3:10; 4:21). They needed to be taught that regeneration is God's work, not theirs.

If these two nice kids had been taught these things, they might still have grown up, gone off to college, and abandoned any walk with Christ, while maintaining their morality. But they wouldn't be deceived into thinking that they were Christians. They would know that they were just nice kids, and nothing more. On the other hand, this teaching might have been used by the Spirit to prick their consciences, awaken them from complacency, and bring them to a vital profession of faith in Christ.

WHY THE DOCTRINE OF REGENERATION MATTERS FOR CHURCHES

But the doctrine of regeneration doesn't just impact how we understand an individual's conversion. Regeneration has a corporate dimension, too.

Consider Ezekiel 36:26–28 again. The "you" throughout these verses is plural, better translated in southern English as "y'all." The result of the Spirit's regenerating work is a people living together under God's rule. The Spirit doesn't simply make me a singular new creation. He makes me part of God's new creation people. He inscribes God's rule on my heart, teaching me about love for neighbor and love for my brothers and sisters in Christ especially. He teaches me that my life with God includes a life with God's people, in the corporate worship and common life of the church.

This is why John can say that you're a liar if you claim to love God but don't love your brother (1 John 4:20). Or why Paul can say that we, Jew and Gentile, have already been made one new man (Eph. 2:13–16). Regeneration gives us a heart not only for God, but also for God's people.

A local church should be a community of new creatures. Through our love and obedience, we give powerful testimony to the radical truth of the gospel. The world can write off a single Christian as an aberration. Put two or three Christians together, and it's harder to write them off. Put five, ten, fifty, a hundred Christians living together in gracious, loving community, and you have a message that cannot be ignored.

Unfortunately, the opposite is also true. When churches look more like the world than Christ, we effectively preach a different gospel. More than likely it will be the gospel of nice.

So what can we do to make sure that our community is a regenerate community, one that together proclaims the power of the gospel of Jesus Christ to make men and women new? Here are a few suggestions:

- *Pay attention to membership.* We don't want regenerate attendance. In fact, we want as many non-Christians as possible to attend. Rather, we want regenerate church membership, because our members officially speak for the church in the world.
- *Conduct membership interviews.* The elders of the church should conduct membership interviews, not to determine how good someone is, but to listen for the evidence of the new birth.
- *Celebrate examples of repentance, not morality.* When members have a chance to hear one another's testimonies in public—when it's normal to confess sin and receive forgiveness—the model of discipleship shifts from self-righteousness to Christlikeness.
- *Practice church discipline.* The goal of corrective church discipline is not to exclude bad people. Nobody should be excluded merely for sinning. Church discipline happens when a professing believer is confronted with sin and refuses to repent. That's not the nature of somebody made new.
- *Keep baptism, church membership, and the Lord's Supper connected.* These are not three separate, independent

29

practices, but three different angles on the same reality of regeneration. The criteria for all three are the same—not nice, but repentance and faith.

We must be made new. Through the Spirit and by the gospel, we have been.

2

SAVED, NOT SINCERE

God's Work, Not Ours

I lived in Washington, DC, in 2009, when Arlen Specter, the long-serving Republican senator from Pennsylvania, converted to being a Democrat. It occurred just before he was faced with a difficult Republican primary challenge, and it wasn't the first time Specter had changed parties in order to win an election.

Two years earlier and on the other side of the Atlantic, Tony Blair announced he was converting to Roman Catholicism just after he stepped down as Britain's prime minister. It was a convenient time to do so since a prime minister is responsible for selecting the archbishop of Canterbury (who leads the Church of England). And selecting the head of a church to which you don't belong is not only awkward; it also raises constitutional questions.

It's hard not to be cynical about such conversions. Both seemed calibrated to the political demands of the moment.

Cynicism is typical these days when it comes to stories of conversion, especially religious ones. They often seem like politically expedient changes of allegiances rather than true changes of the heart. Europe converted at the point of a Roman sword. The so-called Rice Christians of Asia converted for other material benefits. Islam grew in similar fashion. Hinduism and Buddhism advanced on the Indian subcontinent through political and military means.

In response, evangelical Christians since at least the Second Great Awakening (1790s–1850s) have emphasized not just "professions of faith" but the sincerity of the faith professed. Sincerity, after all, would seem to mark the difference between the hypocrite and the genuinely converted. As Fanny Crosby so memorably put it, "The vilest offender who *truly* believes, that moment from Jesus a pardon receives."[1] And typically, sincere faith was demonstrated through some emotion or visible action—raising a hand or walking an aisle, combined with tears of joy and repentance.

HOW SINCERE IS SINCERE ENOUGH?

This was my own experience of conversion growing up. I was raised in gospel-preaching churches in the Deep South where conversion almost always occurred at the end of the service in response to the altar call. Much like Billy Graham at the end of his televised crusades, the preacher would call for a response, lead us in a final hymn, maybe several times, and wait for someone to respond. My own response came at a Sunday evening service when I was in second grade. It had all been arranged in advance. Nevertheless, it was terrifying and exhilarating to walk that aisle, shake the preacher's hand, and hear him confidently pronounce that I was now a child of God.

One result of such a conversion experience is a sense of uncertainty as to whether it was real. And so I found myself regularly witnessing another ritual. Our youth choir often visited various churches. Most nights we would sing the final anthem repeatedly as the local pastor waited for a response. Yet almost without fail, more members of the youth choir would walk forward than anyone else on the final night's altar call. The older kids would lead in coming forward to rededicate their lives to Jesus.

Just in case we hadn't been sincere back when we were barely out of kindergarten, just in case our adolescent sins called our childhood professions into question, my fellow teen choristers and I wanted to make sure that no one, least of all ourselves, had any reason to question the earnestness of our faith. So with tears and hugs we crowded the platform, renewing our conversions.

Yet does an emphasis on sincerity really answer the charge that religious conversion is nothing more than a socially convenient change of allegiances? Is there nothing to distinguish Christian conversion from conversion to a political party, or vegetarianism, or some other lifestyle choice?

The Bible's first word on conversion has nothing to do with the sincerity of believers, though we must be sincere. Its first word is about the activity of God who intervenes in our lives. We become new creatures with new natures when God acts upon us. The Bible doesn't say, "Be sincere"; it says, "Be saved" (e.g., Acts 2:21).

But saved from what? Saved how and why? Saved to what and for what purpose? We'll spend the chapter answering

33

those questions. But again, we should not only be interested in getting our doctrine right, but also in getting our church practices right. The church is the company of the saved, not merely the sincere.

SAVED *FROM* GOD'S WRATH

Paul tells us in Ephesians 2 that we are dead in our trespasses and sins. That's why we must be made new, and not just be nice, as we thought about in the last chapter. But not only are we dead in the sense that we are unable to change, but we are also under God's condemnation. We are "by nature children of wrath," God's wrath.

Remember, God created us in his image to live like sons— "chips off the old block," as they say. But we turned in on ourselves and pursued our own glory. Instead of acting like sons of the King, we tried to overthrow the King and so became children of wrath.

It's popular to think of God's judgment of sinners in hell as God giving us what we ask for—life without God. It's true that hell is the absence of God's love. But hell is also the presence of God in his justice, measuring out to sin what it deserves. And it is this, the wrath of God, from which we must be saved.

- "You will make them as a blazing oven when you appear. The LORD will swallow them up in his wrath, and fire will consume them." (Ps. 21:9)
- "According to their deeds, so will he repay, wrath to his adversaries, repayment to his enemies." (Isa. 59:18)
- "Put to death therefore what is earthly in you: sexual immorality, impurity, passion, evil desire, and covetous-

ness, which is idolatry. On account of these the wrath of God is coming." (Col. 3:5–6)

Since God is good, he will pay back injustice and sin what it deserves. And we all have sinned.

This has enormous implications for our preaching. For the gospel to make sense, we must preach the justice and wrath of God. Too easily, however, churches downplay these basic truths and so change the gospel. It's hard to talk about hell and God's wrath. It is much easier to talk about being saved from purposeless lives, low self-esteem, or unhappiness. So we treat Jesus as the solution to a subjective, internal problem. Come to Jesus; he'll give you purpose and meaning. The trouble is, subjective problems can be solved through subjective solutions. I might choose Jesus to gain a sense of purpose, but my friend down the street sincerely chooses a career. Who's to say which is better? It's all subjective.

When we fail to preach the justice of God and downplay his wrath, we are talking about some other gospel. We have changed it from an objective rescue to a subjective path to personal fulfillment.

Faithfully proclaiming the wrath of God is no easy task. But churches today should consider how they can make God's good, judicial opposition to sin meaningful to modern ears. In our evangelism, we might begin with whatever sense of moral outrage already exists in our culture, and move from there to God's outrage at our sin. In our children's Sunday school classes and youth groups, we must reinforce the lesson that God's wrath, rather than our subjective unhappiness, is our greatest problem. In our discipling, we need to look for opportunities to teach a biblical understanding of the goodness of authority. In our teaching generally, we must observe that God's judgment affirms and secures ultimate human worth. As Bruce Waltke observes, "People deny the doctrine of final judgment because they do not want to give this life such dignity that decisions now affect an eternal future in a decisive and definitive way."[2] But this is precisely the dignity that God gives us and that his wrath reflects.

The wrath of God, in short, is not the marginal concern of a few verses. It's central to Christian worldview formation. If we do not give ourselves to making the bad news meaningful, then the good news will not be meaningful either.

SAVED *BY* GOD'S GRACE

If we are to be saved from God's wrath, it will have to be by God's grace. Paul again from Ephesians 2 says: "For by grace you have been saved through faith. And this is not your own doing; it is the gift of God" (v. 8).

We talk about "saying grace" before a meal. But really, no one can "say grace." We can only receive grace, because grace is a gift. By definition, gifts are not deserved (that's what we call *wages*), and cannot be demanded (that's what we call *rights*). They can only be given or received. The incredible gift of grace that Paul has in mind is God's gift of the forgiveness of sins, purchased by Christ's substitutionary sacrifice on the cross. Because Christ exhausted God's wrath for the sins of those he represents, the Father graciously gives salvation to all those who repent and believe.

The fact of God's grace challenges the moralism that suggests we can clean ourselves up for God. It attacks the pride that thinks God could never forgive me or, conversely, has no need to forgive me. It also puts faith in its place.

Let's think about that last point. Paul says that we are saved by grace through faith. Grace is what saves. Faith is the instrument, which means that we're not saved by faith. Rather, we're saved by grace, and faith receives that grace. Faith trusts that gift. This is why Martin Luther emphasized the fact that we are saved *through* faith alone. The Roman Catholic Church taught that God's grace was received only as we cooperated with God in doing good works, particularly in receiving the Mass. But Luther taught that it is faith alone without the cooperation of good works that receives God's grace. So to be clear, faith does not save. Grace does.

But what happens when we think faith saves us? Sincerity becomes paramount. We begin to think of faith as a single act—a prayer prayed, a decision made, a card signed, a hand raised—rather than as a whole-life orientation. The trouble is, we can never be sure if we were sincere enough. So insecurity follows, and a culture of rededication develops. Anxious children pray "the prayer" over and over. Youth rededicate themselves at every youth retreat. Adults do the same. All are hoping that this time the expression of faith will be sincere enough.

We will discuss faith further in the next chapter, but it's worth emphasizing now that faith isn't an emotion God evaluates by its intensity. Faith is trust, and it's only as good as the object of its trust. So the question isn't "Did you truly believe?" as Fanny Crosby implied. It's "Who did you believe in?"

37

I fear many of our evangelical churches have created a generation of anxious Christians who constantly inspect their faith. Instead churches must point continually to God in Christ, who is good and generous and amazingly gracious. We trust him and his grace for our salvation, not the strength of our emotions.

SAVED *BECAUSE* OF GOD'S LOVE

Why does God save sinners? Because he loves them. Hear Ephesians 2 again: "But God, being rich in mercy, because of the great love with which he loved us, even when we were dead in our trespasses, made us alive together with Christ—by grace you have been saved" (vv. 4–5; see also Titus 3:4–5).

This is the way it always is in Scripture. God's love appears despite our sin and rebellion. Paul elsewhere says: "But God shows his love for us in that while we were still sinners, Christ died for us" (Rom. 5:8). It's not so much, "And so God loves you." It's always, "But God loves you."

The language of God's love is the language of God's choice, his election. God chooses to love. He doesn't have to love us. In fact, by all rights, he shouldn't love us. But he does.

God's love for us isn't on a whim. It's not a last-minute, off-the-cuff love, like a husband suddenly remembering an upcoming wedding anniversary: "Oh, my goodness, my anniversary's coming up. What shall I do?" God's a far better lover than that. From before the foundations of the world God chose to love his people. He planned how he would express that love through the lavish grace of the gospel. He left nothing to chance. Then he executed his plan of love at incredible cost to himself.

If one of my children came to me and said, "Dad, I want you to love me, so I'm going to be especially good today," I would be hurt. "Don't you understand me or my love for you?" I would say. "I don't love you because you're good. I love you because you're mine." God, likewise, doesn't love us because we love and obey him. In fact, we don't! God loves us because he loves us (see Deut. 7:7–8). He loves us because he's chosen us and we are his.

If we turn this around, so that God loves us because we chose and love him, Christianity becomes a religion of self-salvation. The message is that God is obligated to save us because of our love, our choice, our sincerity. Our faith, not his love, becomes the deciding factor. And we introduce pride into the heart and soul of our churches. The gospel has been turned on its head.

God saves us not because of who we are, but despite of it. Why? Because he loves us.

SAVED *INTO* GOD'S PEOPLE

When God saves us, he brings us into a relationship with himself. But not only that, he also brings us into a community.

- "And I have other sheep that are not of this fold. I must bring them also, and they will listen to my voice. So there will be one flock, one shepherd." (John 10:16)
- "He has delivered us from the domain of darkness and transferred us to the kingdom of his beloved Son." (Col. 1:13)

- "But you are a chosen race, a royal priesthood, a holy nation, a people for his own possession." (1 Pet. 2:9)
- "Once you were not a people, but now you are God's people; once you had not received mercy, but now you have received mercy." (1 Pet. 2:10)

Subjects of a kingdom; members of a priesthood; citizens of a nation; a people; part of a flock—different images, but the same idea. God saves us one by one, but he brings us into relationship with each other. This is part of what it means to be saved. Being reconciled to God means being reconciled to God's people, like an adopted child finding him or herself not just with new parents but with new siblings. Notice, for instance, the parallel sentence structure in 1 Peter 2:10 above: *becoming a people* comes with *receiving mercy*.

From the garden, to Abraham and his descendants, to Israel, to the church, to the New Jerusalem, God has always worked to save a people for his Son.

The corporate nature of our salvation is wonderfully demonstrated in Ephesians 2. Having laid out God's gracious act of personal salvation in verses 1–10, Paul then explains the corporate significance of our salvation in verses 11–22. Christ "has made" both Jew and Gentile "one." Notice the past tense. It was done at the cross. Christ has "broken down in his flesh the dividing wall of hostility" (v. 14). He created in himself "one new man in place of the two, so making peace" (v. 15). He did this so that he "might reconcile us both to God in one body through the cross, thereby killing the hostility" (v. 16). As a result, believers who once belonged to warring groups "are no longer strangers and aliens" but "are fellow citizens with the saints and members of the household of God" (v. 19). Now the church, "being joined together, grows into a holy temple in the Lord" and is "a dwelling place for God by the Spirit" (vv. 21, 22).

The same cross-work that reconciled us to God simultaneously reconciled us to each other. Christ united our cases before the bar of God's justice in himself. One representative, one substitutionary sacrifice, for "one new man in place of the two" (v. 15). On the other side of the cross, that reconciliation continues. Peace reigns because both "have access in one Spirit to the Father" (v. 18). This is how profoundly corporate our salvation is. We are "one new man," implying a new race of Adam and Eve's. We are "members of the household of God" (v. 19) drawing on the Abrahamic family imagery of Genesis 12. We are "fellow citizens with the saints" (v. 19), drawing on Israel's kingdom imagery in Exodus 19. We are a "holy temple in the Lord" and a "dwelling place for God by the Spirit" (vv. 21, 22), drawing on God's promise throughout Scripture to dwell with his people.

This isn't aspirational. Paul is not instructing us *to become* this kind of community. He's declaring that this is what God *has already accomplished* through Christ's work. The only command in the entire section is the command to "remember" what God has already done. He has saved us into his covenant community.

The commands follow two chapters later. In Ephesians 4, Paul commands us to bear with one another in love and to maintain the unity of the Spirit in the bond of peace (vv. 2–3).

After all, he says, there is one body, one Spirit, one Lord, one faith, one baptism, and one God who is over all and through all and in all (vv. 4–6).

God has made us one, so we must act as one.

What does the corporate nature of our conversion mean practically? At the very least, it reconnects conversion with church membership. I'll always be grateful for a New England church and its youth ministry that was instrumental in my wife's salvation. They patiently shared the gospel with her, discipled her, baptized her. But, regrettably, they never talked to her about joining the church.

Church membership does not save us. And yet, we can't escape the fact that when people in the New Testament believed, they were added to churches (Acts 2:41, 47; 5:14; 11:21–26; 14:21–23). That wasn't optional; it was inevitable. The apostles taught that it is through the local church that we experience the reality of the universal church to which Christians have been joined in Christ. Notice the progression in Ephesians 2:19–22. Paul observes in verses 19 and 21 that we are *all* fellow citizens and a holy temple in the Lord. Then in verse 22 he turns and refers specifically to the local Ephesian church: "you also are being built together into a dwelling place for God by the Spirit." It's as if Paul is saying: what God has done in *all* of us he is now doing *in you* specifically and concretely. The universal shows up—puts on flesh—in the local.

A familiar logic is at work here. We teach from the New Testament that those who have been *declared* righteous in Christ must *pursue* righteousness in their daily lives. Likewise, those who have been *declared* members of Christ's body must *pursue* membership with an actual group of Christians, a visible local church. If you don't pursue (local and visible) membership, are you really a (universal and invisible) member? Who's to say?

This much should be clear by now: insofar as our salvation involves a corporate dimension, a book on the doctrine of conversion must also be a book on the church.

SAVED *FOR* GOD'S GLORY

Ultimately, the purpose of our salvation is not our salvation. The purpose of our salvation is God's glory. "For my own sake, for my own sake, I do it," God says of his plan of salvation through the prophet Isaiah. "My glory I will not give to another" (Isa. 48:11). He says the same thing through the prophet Ezekiel. Speaking of the promised new covenant, God declares, "It is not for your sake, O house of Israel, that I am about to act, but for the sake of my holy name" (Ezek. 36:22).

This is why God has acted through his Son. Ephesians 2 shows us God's individual and corporate work of salvation, as we have considered throughout this chapter. Yet Ephesians 1 shows us the motive: "for the praise of his glory" (vv. 12, 14). And Ephesians 3 shows us that it is not just our individual salvation that brings God glory. It's *our* salvation. His intent was that now, "through the church, the manifold wisdom of God should be made known to the rulers and authorities in the heavenly places" (v. 10). This was God's "eternal purpose" (v. 11).

This new man, the church, is unlike anything the world has ever seen. Its unity is not based on ethnicity, or culture, or class, but on a person—Jesus Christ, who is the revelation of the wisdom of God (1 Cor. 1:22–30; Col. 2:2–3). Now, in Christ, the church becomes the revelation of God's wisdom to the watching cosmos.

By ourselves, you and I cannot reveal the wisdom of how God has reconciled people to himself and to one another. It takes a local church, where one-time enemies practice loving and forgiving one another, even when they can find lots of reasons not to do so.

When we misunderstand the purpose of our salvation, however, we get into trouble. If we think Jesus saved us to make us happy, fulfilled, or prosperous, we will be tempted to abandon Jesus when those things don't immediately show up on our doorstep. Instead of thinking that salvation is about God's glory, we will assume that the Christian life is all about us, our gifts, calling, and how we can be fulfilled. The local church will become a stage for our potentiality, an arena for our gifts, an audience for our vanity.

But everything changes when we understand that our salvation is about God's glory. No longer is the Christian life about asserting "my Christian rights"; it's about laying down my life to serve others. No longer is the church an outlet for my calling and gifts; it's a community where God's grace is displayed. The mystery is that the "happy, fulfilled life" comes when we stop pursuing *it*, and instead pursue *God* and find in his glory the satisfaction we were made for.

We are saved not by sincerity. Not by intense feelings. Not by loving God or doing any good work. We are saved by God's gracious work in Christ. When our churches understand and live this out together, we show the whole world that Christian conversion is not like changing political parties or denominations. It's not a mere change of mind or feeling. Christian conversion is a rescue. It's a rescue from death to life, from wrath to forgiveness, from enslavement to freedom. And it's God's rescue. Only he can do it.

The hymn writer Charles Wesley put it so well: "Long my imprisoned spirit lay, fast bound in sin and nature's night. Thine eye diffused a quickening ray; I woke, the dungeon flamed with light. My chains fell off. My heart was free. I rose, went forth and followed thee."[3]

Conversion is first God's act, before it is ever ours. We must *be saved*, and through Christ we are.

But conversion is also our act. We rise, go forth, and follow. And it is to our responsibility that we now turn.

3

DISCIPLES, NOT DECISIONS

The Character of Our Response

When I was eighteen years old, I became a Boston Red Sox fan. Having grown up in a state that didn't have a Major League Baseball team, I hadn't developed a local loyalty and just followed the game generally. It dawned on me that I'd enjoy it more if I became a fan of one team. So I sat down with the sports page, studied the box scores and standings, and decided to become a Red Sox fan. It was a lifestyle choice, really.

Thirty years later, I'm still a Red Sox fan. But I'm not sure all my fellow fans would agree. It's not that I follow other teams. It's simply that life is full and busy, and I no longer have time to watch the games on TV, pore over box scores, or keep up with the trades and the prospects. If they make it into the postseason, I'll probably watch, unless I have a meeting, or one of my kids needs help with homework, or my wife needs help with something.

The decision I made stands, but there's not much to show for it these days other than the decision itself.

For many people today, especially in the West, religious conversion is like my decision to become a Red Sox fan. I don't mean to make religious conversion as trivial as picking a baseball team. But in our culture, personal choice is at the heart of both. It's a lifestyle decision.

Within most of evangelical Christianity, this decision is attached to the doctrine of eternal security. "Once saved, always saved," people say. The important thing is making that decision. So just make it, regardless of what you do with the rest of your life.

Recently a man came to my office to talk. I learned that he had made a decision for Jesus years before, as a youth. It was sincere and heartfelt. But like me and the Red Sox, life had become busy. Marriage, work, kids, and the house all kept him away from church and personal spiritual disciplines. No one would know he was a Christian unless he told them. He admitted that he was an alcoholic, and though he'd been sober for a number of years, he'd recently started drinking again.

He came to talk because he had heard a funeral sermon I had given in which I explained that Christ's forgiveness belonged to all those who turn away from their sin and put their trust in Christ and follow him. Just as Jesus did in Mark 1, I'd offered the hope of the gospel to all who "repent and believe" (Mark 1:15). What disturbed him was the idea that being a Christian meant repentance and following. His decision years earlier had been sincere, but perhaps he wasn't a Christian after all. He hadn't really followed. Could I say anything that would help?

Is our role in conversion just "making a decision"? Is that the same thing as what Jesus calls repenting and believing? Given that eternity is at stake, we want to get conversion right, and understand what it means to repent and believe.

A MODEL CONVERSION

In chapters 1 and 2, I made the case that conversion is fundamentally and first a divine work. God must make us new. He must regenerate us. He must act to save. He must justify and forgive and unite us to himself and his people.

But the Bible clearly teaches that conversion is our work too. We have a role to play. God doesn't make anyone a Christian against his will. We must respond to the message of the gospel and become Christians. The biblical language for our response is what I preached in that funeral sermon: everyone must repent of their sins and believe the good news of Jesus Christ.

If we want to know how to become Christians, Paul tells us to look at the Thessalonians. They did it right. Their model can be copied by others. Paul doesn't use the words *repent and believe*, but that's exactly what the Thessalonians did. Paul says to the Thessalonians:

> Our gospel came to you not only in word, but also in power and in the Holy Spirit and with full conviction. . . . And you became imitators of us and of the Lord, for you received the word in much affliction, with the joy of the Holy Spirit, so that

you became an example to all the believers in Macedonia and in Achaia. (1 Thess. 1:5–7)

Paul preached God's gospel Word with the power of the Spirit. The Thessalonians were convicted. In spite of affliction, they turned and became imitators of Paul because they knew God's joy. So evident was the change in their lives that they became a model to churches in other nations.

CONVERSION REQUIRES REPENTANCE

To become a Christian, you must repent of your sins. The basic idea of repentance is *to turn*. Notice how the book of Acts uses the word *repentance* and the idea of turning in parallel:

- "Repent therefore, and turn back, that your sins may be blotted out." (Acts 3:19)
- "They should repent and turn to God, performing deeds in keeping with their repentance." (Acts 26:20)

Likewise, when Paul describes the Thessalonians' conversion, he describes a radical turning or reorientation: "you turned to God from idols to serve the living and true God" (1 Thess. 1:9). But their turning was not merely moral or behavioral. It was a reorientation of worship. Their hearts had turned from worshiping idols to worshiping God.

An idol is anything or anyone without which you can't be happy and fulfilled. We can make an idol out of almost anything: sex, money, other people's opinions of us, security, control, convenience. But our all-time favorite idol is self. I am my favorite idol. You are your favorite idol. And we want others to worship our favorite idol too.

We were created to worship, and if we won't worship God, we'll worship something else.

Calling people to repentance, then, means calling for a reorientation of worship. So who or what are we worshiping rather than God? What compels our time and energy, our spending and our leisure? What makes us angry? What gives us hope and comfort? What are our aspirations for our children?

Idols make lots of promises, even though they can't keep them.

FALSE REPENTANCE

Repenting means exchanging our idols for God. Before it's a change in behavior, it must be a change in worship. How different that is from how we often think of repentance.

Too often we treat repentance as a call to clean up our lives. We do good to make up for the bad. We try to even the scale, or even push it back to the positive side. Sometimes we talk about repentance as if it were a really serious, religious New Year's resolution.

- I'm not going to blow up at my kids anymore.
- I'm not ever going to look at pornography again.
- I'm never going to cheat on my hours at work.
- I'm going to stop talking about my boss behind his back.

But even if we clean our behavior up in one area or another, our hearts can still be devoted to our idols.

The Pharisees illustrate this. They were the best-behaved people in Palestine, the kind of people you would have wanted for a neighbor. They never let their kids throw their bikes in your yard. They didn't throw raucous parties and leave cigarette butts in your flowerbed. They always picked up after their dogs. They were upstanding people. But Jesus called them white-washed tombs: clean on the outside, corrupt on the inside (Matt. 23:27). The point is that it's not just bad people who are idolaters. Good, moral, even religious people are idolaters too. Repentance is not the same thing as moral resolve.

Sometimes we talk about repentance as if it's feeling bad or guilty about our behavior. We feel guilty if we're caught. We feel guilty if we're not caught. We feel guilty if we've let someone down, or let ourselves down. There's no question that repentance requires us to be convinced of our guilt. But you can feel guilty and still love the sin you're guilty of. Anyone who's given in to the pull of lust can tell you that. "Like a dog that returns to his vomit is a fool who repeats his folly" (Prov. 26:11). Repentance is not a feeling.

REAL REPENTANCE

Real repentance is a new worship. It looks like a changed life, but that changed behavior results from a change of worship, not the other way around.

Repentance is being convicted by the Holy Spirit of the sinfulness of our sin—not the badness of our deeds but the treachery of our hearts toward God.

Repentance means hating what we formerly loved and served—our idols—and turning away from them.

Repentance means turning to love God, whom we formerly hated, and serving him instead. It's a new deepest loyalty of the heart.

If repentance really is a change of worship, then our churches must not pressure people to make hasty, ill-considered "decisions" for Jesus, and then offer them quick assurance. Instead, we must call people to repent. When we separate repentance from conversion, either because we think it can come later or we fear scaring people off, we reduce conversion to bad feelings or moral resolve. Worse, we risk assuring a "convert" that he is right with God when in fact he is not. It's almost like giving someone a vaccine against the gospel.

You know how a vaccine works. It uses a defective agent to fool the body into thinking it's been infected so that it will produce antibodies. Then, when the real infection shows up, the body is prepared to fight it off. Likewise, calling people to "make a decision" without calling them to repent not only risks creating a false convert, it also risks vaccinating a person against the real gospel. They think they already have Christianity! Then we double down by saying, "Once saved, always saved."

What does a false convert look like? Often, it is someone who

- is excited about heaven, but bored by Christians and the local church;
- thinks heaven will be great, whether God is there or not;
- likes Jesus, but didn't sign up for the rest—obedience, holiness, discipleship, suffering;

- can't tell the difference between obedience motivated by love and legalism;
- is bothered by other people's sins more than his or her own;
- holds grace cheap and his own comfort costly.

But how does the New Testament describe a genuine Christian? According to 1 John, the genuine Christian is someone who

- loves fellow Christians and the local church because he or she loves God (5:1);
- desires fellowship with God, and not just ease in heaven (1:6–7; 5:1);
- understands that following Jesus means discipleship (1:6);
- obeys God out of love for God (5:2–3);
- is eager to confess and turn away from his or her sin (1:9);
- holds grace costly and his own desires cheap (1:7, 10).

To become a Christian is to take up a life of repentance. Jesus described it as taking up our cross and following him. It begins at a point in time, but it continues in a life of service and love to God. Dietrich Bonhoeffer put it well when he said, "When Christ calls a man, he bids him come and die."[1]

CONVERSION REQUIRES FAITH

If repentance is one side of the coin of conversion, the other side is belief or faith. To become a Christian, you must not only repent, you must also believe the good news about Jesus. "Repent and believe in the gospel," Jesus said (Mark 1:15).

In the model conversion we considered earlier, Paul characterized the Thessalonians as "wait[ing] for his Son from heaven, whom he raised from the dead, Jesus who delivers us from the wrath to come" (1 Thess. 1:10). Notice that Paul summarizes the good news of the gospel in this verse: Jesus, after rising from the dead, promises to deliver us from the wrath to come. In response, the Thessalonians "wait" on Jesus from heaven. There might not be a better description of what it means to believe than to say one *waits* on Jesus from heaven.

WHAT FAITH IS NOT

Faith or belief is more than mentally accepting a set of ideas. Yes, it includes mentally accepting the truth of the gospel. But James warns that the demons believe the truth about God and shudder (James 2:19).

Faith is not reciting a magical verbal formula. Yes, you must "confess with your mouth that Jesus is Lord and believe in your heart that God raised him from the dead," as Paul puts it (Rom. 10:9). But that's not a magical incantation. Say the words, and "presto" you're saved. Unfortunately, evangelicals have asked people to pray the words "Jesus Christ, I'm a sinner, please forgive me of my sins," and then assured them of their salvation, as if the words somehow had power intrinsically attached to them. Roman Catholics have taught that the right person saying the right words turns wine into blood or causes the baptismal water to regenerate an infant. And Muslims will tell you to say three times in Arabic before witnesses, "There is no God but Allah, and Mohammed is his prophet," and you'll become a Muslim. But how can a verbal formula transform a heart that worships idols into a heart that worships God?

Faith is not being spiritual or belonging to a faith community or seeking spiritual direction. It might involve those things. But many people today regard themselves as spiritual or claim to be on a journey, yet have no knowledge of God as he has revealed himself in Jesus Christ.

WHAT FAITH IS

Christian faith is wholehearted trust that God will keep his promises in the gospel. The Thessalonians didn't sign a card or recite a prayer. They began to wait on Jesus, and this showed itself in their lives. The Jews among them stopped depending on Moses and the Law for justification. The Greeks stopped depending on their idols. All of them stopped depending on their wealth. Instead, they started depending on God's gospel promises. Judgment and condemnation did not await them, but eternal life with God did. So they began to live differently. Everyone could see it. Faith changed their lives, because faith not only repeats God's promises back to him in prayer, it also *leans* on those promises.

Recently one of my children became quite ill. We knew in advance that the illness would make him severely disorientated, even delirious, for a time. So while my son was still aware, I looked him in the eye and told him, "No matter what happens, remember two things: I love you, and you can trust me." When the delirium took hold, my son was unable to make sense of what was happening around him. But he would look at me and I would repeat: "I love you. You can trust me." He knew he could lean on these promises.

That is faith. It trusts God, his character, and his love, and so it leans on the promises of the gospel and nothing else. This is why James says faith without works is dead (James 2:17). Real faith leans, and depends, and follows, and works.

WHAT FAITH DO WE TEACH?

What does this understanding of faith mean for the life of the church? First, it impacts what we teach and how we offer assurance. It impacts what we depend upon. Teaching moralism makes us depend on our good deeds. Teaching sincerity makes us depend on emotional experiences and a culture of rededication. Teaching spirituality makes us depend on the fact of a journey and not the hope of the destination. Teaching "decisionism" causes us to depend on that prayer we prayed at children's summer camp or the married couples' retreat.

"Examine yourselves, to see whether you are in the faith," Paul says (2 Cor. 13:5). Paul doesn't tell us to examine past decisions or whether we're feeling spiritual. He instructs Christians to look at life today. Saving faith clings to Christ and doesn't let go. And like repentance, it leaves evidence throughout a believer's life. As churches, we want to look for the current evidence of God's grace in one another's lives and point them out to each other.

WHAT FAITH DO WE OFFER?

Second, understanding biblical faith impacts our evangelism. If evangelism without repentance produces false converts, so does evangelism without a right understanding of faith.

57

Treating faith as mental assent or a verbal creed creates "formal professors," as the Puritans called them. These people can explain the gospel. They agree with it. They have said a prayer. They might have been moved emotionally when they did. But they don't know Jesus or lean on his promises, as revealed in their lives, relationships, and character. As John says, for instance, "If anyone says, 'I love God,' and hates his brother, he is a liar; for he who does not love his brother whom he has seen cannot love God whom he has not seen" (1 John 4:20).

Ever since the Second Great Awakening, evangelicals have characterized conversion as a decision. Raise your hand! Come forward! Come to the altar! What is the fruit of turning conversion into a decision? Churches filled with professing Christians whose lives look no different than the world's. Comparable Christian divorce rates. Rampant materialism. High pornography usage. Church "members" who rarely, if ever, attend. The problem is not that we have Christians in our churches who still sin. Of course we do. The problem is that we have "Christians" in our churches who aren't Christians. But we have given them assurance and told them to never let anyone question it.

To our shame, we boast about these "decisions" and count our evangelism a success. Yet where are the vast majority of those "converts" in a year's time? Why were we so excited? I fear we were excited because they were *our* converts. One thinks of Charles Spurgeon's story about Pastor Roland Hill. A drunken man accosted Pastor Hill one day and said, "Hey, Mr. Hill. I'm one of your converts." Hill replied, "You must be one of mine. You're certainly not one of the Lord's!"[2]

When offices and schools and playing fields are filled with *our* converts, the world replies, "If that's a Christian, why bother with Jesus?"

We can easily harvest, manipulate, and collect decisions. But Jesus told us to go and make disciples. Not decisions, not converts, but disciples—life-long followers who endure hardship, take up their cross, and follow Jesus.

WHAT FAITH DO WE MODEL?

Finally, understanding biblical faith impacts church membership.

We should not set the bar for being a disciple higher than Jesus did, but we shouldn't set it lower either. How did Jesus call people to respond to the gospel? "Repent and believe in the gospel" (Mark 1:14–15). And that's exactly what the first disciples did. They left their former lives and followed Jesus in repentance and faith.

How then did the apostles call people to respond to the gospel? On the day of Pentecost, Peter preached to the crowds in Jerusalem, "Repent and be baptized every one of you in the name of Jesus Christ for the forgiveness of your sins, and you will receive the gift of the Holy Spirit" (Acts 2:38).

Did you notice the change in language? "Repent and believe" became "Repent and be baptized." Peter was not saying baptism saves. Rather, he was saying that faith's way of showing itself is baptism. It's how faith publicly responds and "signs the bottom line," as it were.

Let me back up a second. In Matthew 16 and 18, Jesus confers the authority of the keys of the kingdom on local churches

59

to formally affirm both true confessions of the gospel and true gospel confessors. Then in Matthew 26 and 28, Jesus establishes the Lord's Supper and baptism, which is how churches use the keys and grant assurance to gospel confessors. Baptism is the first word of public assurance that other people agree with your profession. That's why a church baptizes you into the "name" of Father, Son, and Spirit (28:19). "Here's the team jersey!" The Lord's Supper then offers that assurance on an ongoing basis. "Because there is one bread, we who are many are one body, for we all partake the one bread" (1 Cor. 10:17). Participating in the one loaf affirms and reveals who the one body is. A church can also remove its affirmation of someone's profession of faith through church discipline or excommunication, which removes a person from the Lord's Table and membership in the church.

In other words, Jesus did not leave behind a crowd of self-affirming individuals and one-time decision-makers. Rather, he left behind a church with the authority to baptize and give the Lord's Supper, which is another way of saying, he left behind something we call "church membership." Church membership, at its biblical core, is our affirmation and oversight of one another's professions of faith and discipleship to Christ, which we do through baptism and the Supper.

When we baptize people, therefore, it should be the norm that we then take them into membership in our church. It should be the norm, in other words, to keep baptism and the Supper together. One is the front door into the house. The other is the ongoing family meal. Keeping them together is how you do more than affirm one-time decisions; it's how we affirm transformed lives of ongoing repentance. It's how we make sure our corporate affirmations have integrity, and how we fight against false converts and Christian nominalism.

Of course there will be exceptions. Visitors from other churches may visit and join you in the Supper, assuming another gospel-affirming church would affirm their profession as members. Your church is not the only church in the world, after all. And sometimes we might baptize someone and then immediately say goodbye as they leave for another city or country. But those exceptions shouldn't define our normal practice.

The bigger picture is that a faith that identifies with Jesus's death and resurrection cannot be separated from a faith that identifies with Jesus's people. As Gordon Smith puts it, "Conversion is not merely a conversion to Christ; it is also an act of initiation into Christian community. Christian faith is distinctly *social*."[3] True faith therefore unites itself to a local church even as it unites itself to God. After Peter commanded the people to repent and be baptized, we read, "Those who received his word were baptized, and there were added that day about three thousand souls" (Acts 2:41). Added to what? The church in Jerusalem.

GIVING ASSURANCE

A biblical understanding of repentance and faith means churches are called to make disciples, not decisions. The trouble is, our man-fearing and self-sufficient hearts will always be tempted to quickly offer people assurance. But we must be more thoughtful in how we extend assurance.

I once had the opportunity to help with a major evangelistic crusade. In our training, we were taught to tell people that if they would simply say the prayer printed on the card we gave them, they could be assured that they were born again and would spend eternity with God, and to never doubt that truth. My concern with this strategy is twofold. First, it encouraged people to find their assurance in their decision and prayer on that day. But the Bible doesn't instruct us to look back on some decision we once made. It instructs us to examine our lives today, to see if we are in the faith (2 Cor. 13:5). Is there ongoing repentance and faith? To paraphrase John Piper, I don't know I'm alive because I have a birth certificate. I know I'm alive because I'm breathing.[4]

Second, the word of assurance should be given by a church through baptism and membership in a church. This is how Jesus set it up. Let's do evangelistic rallies, but let's also immediately point people to churches. In the life of a church, the word of assurance comes from people who know you, and who will then walk with you over time. It's not that churches will never make mistakes. But that word of assurance, given through the ordinances, should be tied to a community of people living life together.

To be sure, churches cannot presume to see into the heart. But Jesus repeatedly affirmed our ability to make assessments based on the outward, observed life:

- "You will recognize them by their fruits . . . every healthy tree bears good fruit, but the diseased tree bears bad fruit." (Matt 7:16–17)

- "The good person out of his good treasure brings forth good, and the evil person out of his evil treasure brings forth evil." (Matt. 12:35)
- "For out of the heart come evil thoughts, murder, adultery, sexual immorality, theft, false witness, slander." (Matt. 15:19)

We cannot see a tree's roots by looking at the tree. But we can see if it's bearing apples or oranges. We cannot observe the extent to which pride rules a heart or lust dominates the desires. Or greed governs the will. But we can see how a man treats his children and loves his wife. We can know if someone is stealing or committing fraud. These are the visible fruit of an invisible heart.

It is the work of the church to hear professions of faith, to consider such fruit, and to offer assurance to the repentant. It's not that the church isn't a community of sinners. It is. It's that the church is a community of a particular kind of sinners—repentant sinners.

Another word for that is *disciples*.

4

HOLY, NOT HEALED

Implications for the Christian Life

I was born the year before Phil Donahue got his start, and grew up with his show in the background of my childhood. Donahue, if you don't know him, was the first Oprah. Oprah herself said, "If there had been no Phil Donahue show, there would be no Oprah Winfrey show."[1] He was a pioneer. But he was more than that. He, Oprah, Dr. Phil, and others understood something about our culture. As a nation we were moving from a moral to a therapeutic worldview, and these shows reflected that fact and led the way.

The therapeutic attitude is the conviction that our great need as individuals is to learn to love and accept ourselves, to get comfortable in our own skin. When we look for validation from others, all sorts of personal and social maladies result: eating disorders, codependent relationships, drug abuse, abusive marriages . . . the list is endless. But all this is a quixotic quest to find what in the end only we can give to ourselves: unconditional acceptance.

This is where shows like Donahue's came in. He invited

guests to confess behavior that would ordinarily be considered deviant. But the purpose of these on-air confessions was not to obtain forgiveness and absolution. The purpose was to facilitate acceptance, acceptance by the guest himself and—usually—the studio audience. A guest's "coming out" demonstrated radical self-acceptance. Yet the work of these group therapy sessions traveled beyond the television studios into the living rooms of everyone watching. If that person on TV who is more messed up than I am can accept himself, then I can too. The extremes displayed on Donahue and Oprah gave us permission to throw off shame and guilt and finally begin to love ourselves.

Healing comes to the broken, hurting individual by setting her free from other people's standards so that she can accept herself for who she is. Not only that, the therapeutic mind-set also teaches us to accept others for whoever they are. Therapeutic healing leads to happy, well-adjusted people who can say, "I'm okay. You're okay."

Now, Christians since the 1960s have recognized that this message leaves out Jesus. We don't just need to accept ourselves. We need God to accept us. And the good news of the gospel, we reason, is that God not only accepts us and says, "You're okay," he also unconditionally loves us. To change the image, the therapeutic culture may say that our hearts are empty buckets that only we can fill ourselves. But as Christians, we know we can't. Only Jesus can fill our buckets with his infinite love, which never runs out. For many Christians today, that's the good news of Christianity. Jesus fills the void in our hearts. He brings healing to our brokenness.

REAL HEALING IS BEING MADE HOLY

In the first three chapters, I argued that conversion is first and fundamentally God's work in us, but that we also have a role and responsibility. We don't need just a decision, but a complete reorientation of the heart in worship through repentance and faith. In the rest of this book, I will explore the implications of conversion for our lives individually, for our churches, and for our evangelism. If conversion means that we are made new through the sovereign, saving work of God, what difference should that make?

To begin with, it means that we are not healed therapeutically. Instead, we actually become holy.

Now before I dismiss the language of healing, let me be quick to say that healing is one biblical image for salvation. Isaiah declared, "With his wounds we are healed" (Isa. 53:5). And Jesus came to heal the sick, a physical illustration of something bigger. But what the Bible means by healing is different from what our modern, therapeutic culture means. In the Bible, sickness is a consequence of sin and the curse. It's also a picture of our unholy spiritual nature and our inability to please God. Being healed, then, is not at all about coming to peace with ourselves. It's about having our guilt and shame and ultimately the curse removed and being restored to a right relationship with God. In other words, to be healed in Scripture is to be made holy.

What does it mean that Christians are holy? It doesn't mean that Christians are better than others. It doesn't mean we can adopt a "holier-than-thou" attitude. It doesn't mean that we're rule keepers, whether those rules come from the fundamentalist right or the progressive left. Rather, a Christian is holy because he or she has been (1) set apart (2) to a new master (3) with a new love.

Let's look at each of these in turn.

TO BE HOLY IS TO BE SET APART

To be holy is to be set apart.

To make this point, Paul uses an image in his letter to the Colossians that most of us are not accustomed to dealing with: circumcision. Paul writes:

> In [Christ] you were circumcised with a circumcision made without hands, by putting off the body of the flesh, by the circumcision of Christ, having been buried with him in baptism, in which you were also raised with him through faith in the powerful working of God, who raised him from the dead. And you, who were dead in your trespasses and the uncircumcision of your flesh, God made alive together with him, having forgiven us all our trespasses, by canceling the record of debt that stood against us with its legal demands. This he set aside, nailing it to the cross. (Col. 2:11–14)

Paul uses circumcision to describe our conversion: We were dead in our sin. But God made us alive through faith. What's easy to pass over here is the imagery of circumcision. Most of us know what the medical procedure is. We probably know the Israelites practiced it. But I doubt many of us walk around thinking of our conversions with the imagery of foreskin removal.

Paul did. Here's why.

In the Old Testament, God set Abraham and his descendants apart for a special relationship with himself through a covenant. He also gave them a sign of the covenant: circumcision (Gen. 17:11). Circumcision marked Abraham and his descendants as holy—for God's use and under God's blessing. To remain uncircumcised was to be cut off from the covenant relationship (Gen. 17:14).

In his letter to the Colossians, Paul grabs the image of circumcision and applies it to the church. Of course he is not talking about cutting off some skin with a scalpel. He's making an analogy. Just as Abraham's descendants were set apart by God as holy, so everyone united to Christ has been set apart or consecrated by Christ.

Consecration—another word for being set apart—isn't something that characterizes only the really spiritual Christians. There are not two classes of Christians: the really holy ones and the rest of us. All Christians are holy. We have all been circumcised and consecrated in Christ.

What does it look like to be set apart? For Old Testament Israel, circumcision was just the start. You also wore different clothes than everyone else; you ate different food; you organized your fields differently; you put up different decorations on the walls of your house. You even had a different kind of haircut. Imagine going to the barber and asking for the holiness cut! In other words, God intended the set-apartness of an Israelite, which began with circumcision on the eighth day, to manifest itself for the rest of his life, in all of his life, for everyone to see.

For the New Testament Christian, our set-apartness isn't primarily physical, but it is supposed to be visible, and increasingly so, in all of life, for our whole life, for everyone to see. People should see our holiness in our manner of life. Paul moves seamlessly from the gospel and our spiritual circumcision in Colossians 2 to how we should live in Colossians 3:

> If then you have been raised with Christ, seek the things that are above. . . . Set your minds on things that are above, not on things that are on earth. . . .
>
> Put to death therefore what is earthly in you: sexual immorality, impurity, passion, evil desire, and covetousness, which is idolatry . . . put on the new self, which is being renewed in knowledge in the image of its creator . . .
>
> Put on then, as God's chosen ones, holy and beloved, compassionate hearts, kindness, humility, meekness and patience, . . . put on love. (Col. 3:1–2, 5, 10, 12, 14)

I suppose we might say Paul *is* concerned with what we wear. We're to put off our old way of living and to put on the way of Christ. Paul is not slipping back into moralism, as in "Live good lives so God will accept you." He's drawing out the implications of our conversion, our spiritual circumcision.

These visible marks of holiness are how you're supposed to recognize a new creature in Christ when he passes you on the street or moves in next door. It won't be his special clothes or odd diet. It will be the character of his life. And a Christian lives this way not because she's finally learned to love herself, but because God has changed her nature; and by changing

70

her nature he has set her apart for himself. God makes Christians holy.

So what's the difference between a culture's version of therapy or healing and biblical holiness? One says, "You're okay"; the other says, "You've been chosen and set apart." One tells me to love myself and keep my sin because it's all fine; the other says that my ultimate destiny and new self are not to be identified with my sin, so that I must say no to it. One tries to make me feel good about myself; the other orients my life toward God. One is about me and how I feel; the other is about God and his work in my life.

When our churches slip into a therapeutic gospel, we treat the Christian life less as a battle against sin and more as a battle to feel accepted. We stop singing the old hymns about sanctification and perseverance, and sing instead the romanticized lyrics that trade heavily in images of Jesus's closeness, embrace, and tender touch. We regard every exhortation against sin in a sermon as legalistic, incentivized obedience through guilt. We define our relationship wholly in terms of acceptance. We even reshape obedience by the therapeutic imperative. For example, if I can't rationally or emotionally discern how sexual purity or remaining in a difficult marriage is good for *me*, then I might acknowledge that such commands are fine for others, but that God didn't intend me to be unhappy and unfulfilled. To put it in theological terms, the therapeutic gospel teaches us to love the indicatives of the gospel, but to avoid the imperatives of the gospel, and to read both the indicative and the imperative through the lens of my own happiness.

Holiness is not mere rule-keeping or maintaining external codes of morality. It's the freedom of a new nature.

Yes, the flesh is at war with the spirit in each of us (1 Pet. 2:11), and this war will continue until the Lord calls us home. Nevertheless, it is not burdensome to live according to the new nature if you have it. What's burdensome is to live according to a nature that you don't have. In fact, it's worse than burdensome. It's impossible. Could it be that you don't live as if you've been set apart because you haven't been set apart? As one recent writer on holiness has observed:

> Some pollsters and pundits look at the worldliness of the church and conclude that being born again doesn't make a difference in how people live. We should come to the opposite conclusion; namely, that many churchgoers are not truly born again.[2]

TO BE HOLY IS TO BE SET APART TO A NEW MASTER

Why does holiness even matter?

Recently a fellow who attends my church asked me this question. He loves Jesus and appears to lead a holy life. But he comes out of a legalistic background, and having only recently discovered the freedom that salvation is by grace alone, he didn't want talk of holiness and obedience for fear of undermining the gospel. His approach was to trust that God's grace would work things out in his life.

Holiness matters because being "set apart" means being set apart to a new master. That's one of the lessons of Romans 6.

Paul opens the chapter with a milder version of this man's

question: "What shall we say then? Are we to continue in sin that grace may abound?" (v. 1). If we've been totally forgiven and accepted by God because of what Christ has done, why not just go on sinning?

Paul begins his answer by pointing to our baptism: we were buried with Christ in baptism and raised with him from the grave (vv. 2–5). Then he explains what this means. Formerly we were "enslaved to sin" (v. 6) because our nature rules us, and our nature is corrupted by sin. Sin, therefore, was our master.

But now our old self is dead. God gave us new life in Christ, life that was bought at a price. That means we now have a new master, and our lives follow the pattern he set.

In his earthly life, Jesus did not serve sin, but God. For our sakes he "died to sin" and "lives to God" (v. 10). Through our union with Christ by baptism into his death and resurrection, our allegiances have shifted to a new master. We used to offer our bodies in service to sin "as instruments for unrighteousness." But now, as people "who have been brought from death to life," we offer our lives in service to God, as instruments in his hands "for righteousness" (v. 13).

So holiness matters because it reveals who our master is. Christians march to a different drummer. We respond to different commands. And the world notices. They first called us "Christians"—little Christs—as an insult. But it was a name we were only too happy to receive because it shows where our allegiances lie. These different allegiances explain why Christians have always faced persecution. We aren't pursuing the same goals or following the same orders as everyone around us. Our lives don't validate the world, but contradict it. And the world has never taken kindly to being contradicted.

Once again, what's the difference between the therapeutic gospel and the biblical gospel? In the therapeutic gospel, Jesus has come to fill the void in your heart. In the biblical gospel, he has come to establish his lordship over your life.

The therapeutic gospel doesn't deny that Jesus is Lord. It just ignores it. But the effect is the same, because my heart's sovereign need for love and acceptance is left unchallenged. I might confess that Jesus is Lord, but his lordship would never lead me into suffering or persecution. It would never confront my sin, especially through the correction of other Christians. It would never ask me to give up my kids to his service, rather than a respectable career. I remain Lord, and my need to feel safe and loved remains my ruling principle.

Allegiance shows. Jesus said quite bluntly, "No one can serve two masters, for either he will hate the one and love the other, or he will be devoted to the one and despise the other" (Matt. 6:24).

If you are a Christian, your allegiance to Christ will show itself through the way you use your money, your time, your body, your careers, your home. It will show itself in how you love your spouse or children. It will show itself in how you treat Christ's church.

I'm not saying we learn to follow Christ in a day. I genuinely put my faith in Christ as a child. But as I grew up, other things battled for my allegiance: girls, academic success, and a career in medicine, to name a few. By the time I went to college, I knew I had to choose. I'm eternally grateful to God that he grabbed hold of me during my freshman year and would not let me go. Now, thirty years later, I wish I could say that the past three decades have displayed an unbroken, unwavering commitment to Christ. Sadly, I've continued to feel the pull of other masters. Again and again I've had to come back to Romans 6, repent of my double-mindedness, and heed Paul's exhortation to "consider myself dead to sin" and to "present myself to God."

Allegiance to a new master is not a "once and done" act. It's continually tested and continually renewed. Like an enlisted soldier who swore his allegiance when he signed the papers but renews that allegiance every time he salutes a passing officer, so it is with Christians. We signed in our baptism, and Romans 6 tells us to consider the meaning of our baptism daily: we are dead to sin, and alive to God in Christ.

A NEW LOVE

Finally, Christians are holy because they are set apart to a new love.

> Dear friends, let us love one another, for love is from God, and whoever loves has been born of God and knows God. Anyone who does not love does not know God, because God is love. In this the love of God was made manifest among us, that God sent his only Son into the world, so that we might live through him. In this is love, not that we have loved God but that he loved us and sent his Son to be the propitiation for our sins. Beloved, if God so loved us, we also ought to love one another. No one has ever seen God; but if we love one another, God abides in us and his love is perfected in us. (1 John 4:7–12)

How can you be certain that you've been born again? You can tell by who you love. Fundamental to what it means to be fallen, sinful creatures is that we love ourselves rather than God and neighbor. Our hearts are not passive, needy love buckets, looking for love in all the wrong places, as the therapeutic worldview teaches. Our hearts are corrupt. We love ourselves rather than God. We love ourselves rather than our neighbor. When we go looking for love, we prefer the love of people rather than God because people affirm us for who we are in our sin. God may promise to love us despite who we are, but that's not good enough.

When we are converted, consecrated, circumcised, and baptized into the very life of God through Christ, God "lives in us and his love is made complete in us." Our loves change. God gives us a new nature that loves God and loves others. God's love changes us, and the proof is in our self-sacrificing love.

Do you see the problem with turning Jesus's love for me into a therapeutic cure for my brokenness? It's true that Jesus's love fills us in a way nothing else can. But the therapeutic gospel keeps me at the center of my loves, and I will love others only when I feel full. The apostle John says rather this is love: not that Jesus felt full and affirmed and whole, but that he was emptied and hurt and broken and ultimately punished by the wrath of God for our sin. And it's right there in that place Christ loved us the most. Buried and raised with Christ, Christians, too, are called to love God and neighbor even when they don't feel full of God's love.

In the midst of suffering and persecution, we love. When God feels absent, Christians love. When we're sinned against,

Christians love. We don't love because we feel loved. We love because we have been loved, and that love has changed us.

The therapeutic gospel is a half-truth gospel. It tells us that we are loved by God through Christ, and so we've been healed from our emptiness. But the whole truth is so much better. It lifts us out of the petty kingdom of our needy heart, changes us, and sets us apart in the service of the King of love.

Through Christ, you have been declared holy. And by God's grace, that is what you will be.

5

DISTINCT,
NOT DESIGNED

Implications for the Corporate
Life of the Church

Remember before there were designer jeans? You went to the store and bought a generic pair of jeans because that's all there was.

That changed in the mid-1970s. I remember it mattered to the kids at school what the label said on the back of your jeans. Brands became an essential way of saying who you were and which group you belonged to.

Yet the desire to belong to a group wasn't invented in the 1970s. Branding simply gave us a new tool to do what people have been doing for millennia. People have divided themselves one way or another at least since the Tower of Babel. Being with people "like us" makes us feel safe, understood, and appreciated. There's less conflict when we're all the same. So culture divides into class. Class subdivides according to lifestyles. Pretty soon, the concerts and the bowling alley and the shooting range and the churches became filled with "folk like us."

Building on the church-growth theories of missionaries like Donald McGavran, church leaders in the twentieth century discovered they could grow their churches more quickly by dropping the "one size fits all" approach. So began what we might call the designer church movement. These days there are Boomer churches, Gen-X churches, and millennial churches. We have suburban churches complete with theater seating and cup holders as well as gritty urban hipster churches that look like the club down the street. In most cases the goal is to make the church feel less "churchy" and to reach a particular niche market. So programs mirror the natural interests of the target audience. The staff dress like cultural insiders. And to all appearances, the strategy works. The largest churches in America all follow this principle. After all, like attracts like. And birds of a feather really do flock together.

But is it Christian?

The biblical doctrine of conversion actually teaches something different. It teaches that Christians and churches should be distinct, not designed. We should be set apart from the world, not conformed to it. And it's a church's distinctness that gives credence to the truth of our message.

Now as a child of fundamentalism, I want to be quick to acknowledge that this distinctness has often been pursued in wrong-headed ways. We've worn different clothes, avoided cards and movies, looked down our noses at non-Christians, and then taken a foolish pride in those things as marks of our holiness. Yet Scripture isn't interested in our styles and preferences, but in the quality of our lives and our loves. The doctrine of conversion means that a church should be a distinct community.

A DISTINCT COMMUNITY

Throughout the Bible God calls his people to be distinct. From the garden, to Noah's Ark, to God's people in Egypt and the wilderness, to Israel in the land, to Peter who describes the church as "sojourners and exiles" (1 Pet. 2:11), the Scriptures call God's people to distinct lives, even as they invite the nations to join them. The trouble is, too often we want to be like the world. Old Testament Israel wanted a king so that they could be like the nations. The Corinthian church wanted to show how culturally relevant and hip they were with their fancy oratory. Today's evangelicals worry about whether the world thinks we're smart enough, politically astute enough, culturally sophisticated enough.

But Paul has a different agenda:

Do not be unequally yoked with unbelievers. For what partnership has righteousness with lawlessness? Or what fellowship has light with darkness? What accord has Christ with Belial? Or what portion does a believer share with an unbeliever? What agreement has the temple of God with idols? For we are the temple of the living God; as God said,

"I will make my dwelling among them and walk
among them,
and I will be their God,
and they shall be my people.

> Therefore go out from their midst,
>> and be separate from them, says the Lord,
> and touch no unclean thing;
>> then I will welcome you,
> and I will be a father to you,
>> and you shall be sons and daughters to me,
> says the Lord Almighty."

Since we have these promises, beloved, let us cleanse ourselves from every defilement of body and spirit, bringing holiness to completion in the fear of God. (2 Cor. 6:14–7:1)

Paul piles up a number of images that all serve to clearly demark the line between the church and the world. The local church is a "fellowship," a "yoking" together of people who are in the "light" instead of "darkness," in "Christ" instead of "Belial," "believers" not "unbelievers" characterized by "righteousness" not "lawlessness."

Paul is not talking about who can show up at church meetings. He's talking about the Corinthian church's covenantal commitments to one another, and how they identify with Christ and one another. Together they are "the temple of God."

A church is a group of Christians who have yoked themselves to each other in Christ (see Matt. 11:29–30). They are not to remove themselves from the world of unbelievers or be weird for weird's sake. But the members of a church should be identifiably separate, set apart and distinct, in the fear God.

Yet how easy it is to deceive ourselves that we're trying to be relevant and accessible, when in fact we're looking for approval. So we design our churches in ways that will draw a crowd, but in the process we contradict the power and the message of the gospel we preach. We expose our true confidence and let the world shape the church.

What should our distinct communities look like? According to Scripture, our distinctness should consist of holy lives and self-sacrificing love.

HOLY LIVES

The apostle Peter calls us to holiness. He writes, "Do not be conformed to the passions of your former ignorance, but as he who called you is holy, you also be holy in all your conduct, since it is written, 'You shall be holy, for I am holy.'" (1 Pet. 1:14–16). This is what God requires of those who have been "ransomed" with "the precious blood of Christ" (vv. 18, 19).

What does that mean for a local church corporately? It means our whole community should look radically different from the surrounding culture, not just because we are each privately following Christ, but because we take the witness of the whole quite seriously. We understand that our lives aren't our own anymore, that we belong to each other because we all belong to Christ. Sure enough, Peter goes on to describe us as a "holy nation," foreigners and exiles who "keep [their] conduct among the Gentiles honorable, so that when they speak against you as evildoers, they may see your good deeds and glorify God on the day of visitation" (1 Pet. 2:9, 11–12).

Taking holiness seriously as a church also means practicing corrective church discipline. Paul, for instance, tells the Corinthian church to put a man out of their fellowship who was living in a way that even the world found scandalous

(1 Corinthians 5). He wants them to remove the man from the church for the sake of the man (so he'll repent), for the sake of weaker sheep (so they won't be led astray), and for the sake of the world outside (so they'll trust the converting power of the gospel). He doesn't want anyone to be confused about what it means to be a Christian. He knows the problem isn't sin. Genuine Christians sin. The problem is unrepentant sin in Christians who, when confronted with their sin, continue in it. Doing so is utterly inconsistent with the claim to be a follower of Christ. Paul knows the credibility of the church's entire message was on the line.

Sometimes love has to say hard things. We cannot claim to know the heart, but we can help one another fight for holiness by correcting unrepentant sin. We ordinarily do this through private correction, once in a while through public admonishment, and once in a very great while through excluding someone from the Lord's Supper and membership for persistent unrepentant sin. Biblical church discipline is not legalistic or judgmental. It's loving, both to the one confronted and to the watching world, which needs to understand that through the gospel, Jesus Christ actually changes our lives.

SELF-SACRIFICING LOVE

Finally, our churches should be distinct communities by being loving communities. Jesus said, "A new commandment I give to you, that you love one another: just as I have loved you, you also are to love one another. By this all people will know that you are my disciples, if you have love for one another" (John 13:34–35).

Jesus tells us our witness depends on loving each other as he has loved us. How has he loved us? By going to the cross. How shall we love one another? By forgiving one another and laying down our lives for each other.

As the gospel story unfolds in Acts, we learn that this mutual love in Christ is not just for fellow Jewish Christians. Christ's love extended to the Gentiles as well. Paul later observes that through the love and unity of Jew and Gentile as one new humanity through the gospel, God's incredible wisdom and power and grace is put on display for the universe (Eph. 3:10).

After all, it doesn't take God's wisdom and power to love people who are like us. That's easy. Jesus observes that even tax collectors have friends (Matt. 5:46). But Christ loved us while we were still his enemies. And loving like Christ means loving those who are radically different from us, which does require the power of the gospel.

Recently our church baptized an aesthetically sophisticated art professor. Art professors are not exactly our demographic, which skews toward blue collar and pop culture. In his membership interview, I asked him why he'd chosen our church. He admitted that he felt culturally distant in some ways. But having just become a Christian, he knew he didn't need people just like him. He'd had that his whole life. He needed people with whom he shared Christ, and loved him for no other reason.

Because of Christ, I have more in common with a retired widow in my church than I do with a non-Christian dad who is my age and likes to hike and camp like me. Because of Christ, a white, middle-aged businessman has more in common with a young Native American woman in his church than he does with a non-Christian member of his Rotary Club. To the world, this seems crazy, but it's true. And the only way to explain it is the gospel of Jesus Christ, which makes us one.

The loving oneness we share in the gospel is the crucial difference between a club and a church, and why we should not design our churches to resemble clubs. Clubs, affinity groups, and designer churches are places where "folk like us" get together to enjoy our commonality. But a real church is one where we don't need to have anything in common other than Christ in order to radically love one another.

Practically, what does this look like? It looks like churches going out of their way to find and welcome Christian international students and immigrants. It looks like wealthier white churches helping and learning from less wealthy ethnic churches. It looks like planting churches at our own cost, rather than multiplying services and campuses for our own gain. It looks like a small group of young single men visiting an elderly stroke victim from their church on a Friday night to sing hymns and encourage her. That really happened in my church. The attending nurse asked if this older woman was famous because of all the visitors she had received. The young men replied, "No, she's not famous. She's a member of our church."

It's comparatively easy to attract Boomers if you're a Boomer church, Gen-Xers if you're an Xer church, hipsters if you're a hipster church. Or you can divide into multiple services with multiple styles so that everyone can find people just like them. But isn't this what clubs are for? Who needs the power of the gospel for any of this?

The power and truth of the gospel are displayed when churches live differently (pursuing holiness), love differently (forgiving our enemies), and look different (multiethnic, multigenerational, multi-economic). We testify to Jesus and his good news when our community of love cuts across the lines of growth the world expects, a community that can be explained only by the gospel that changes lives.

6

SUMMON, DON'T SELL

Implications for Our Evangelism

In 1892, the elegant and grand Marshall Field & Company department store opened in Chicago. Each morning, the founder and namesake toured his store to make certain business was running as it should. One morning, he saw one of his managers arguing with a customer. He asked the manager, "What are you doing here?" The manager replied, "I am settling a complaint." Field snapped back, "No, you're not. Give the lady what she wants."[1]

In the emerging free marketplace of America, Field was one of the first to realize that the customer was king. Previously, the adage *caveat emptor* ("buyer beware") defined the relationship between buyer and seller. Now, a new principle began to drive the incredible expansion of American prosperity: "The customer is always right."

In the twentieth century, marketing came of age, and sales was transformed. Sales began to focus less on the product (Model T: "High priced quality in a low priced car") and more on the customers, their desires, and even their sense of who they were ("Not your father's Oldsmobile"). For instance, in the 1960s Pepsi began to exploit the so-called generation gap by claiming their product was for the "Pepsi Generation." This approach would eventually be called lifestyle marketing.

Not surprisingly, it didn't take long for these consumer-focused strategies to make their way from the commercial marketplace to the religious marketplace. In the latter half of the twentieth century, people worried less about "salvation" or "forgiveness." They felt other needs: for happiness, purpose, fulfillment, freedom from addiction, a satisfying sex life. So churches responded with "felt needs" evangelism. You don't change the gospel; you just market it as giving people what they want, like fulfillment and freedom, rather than empha-sizing what they don't want, like forgiveness. One well-known evangelical described the background thinking here: "It is my deep conviction that anybody can be won to Christ if you dis-cover the key to his or her heart . . . it is sometimes difficult to discover. But the most likely place to start is with the person's felt needs."[2]

And it works, at least in America. Churches are filled with people who are saved from purposeless, unfulfilling lives. But are they saved from God and his judgment?

The biblical doctrine of conversion has enormous impli-cations for our approach to evangelism. If conversion is the result of God's work of giving us new hearts that repent and believe the gospel, then evangelism is not a sales method. It is not about identifying felt needs and shaping the gospel product accordingly. What would we think of an ambassador sent by a president to warn a hostile nation, but who only emphasized what he thought the hostile nation wanted to hear? Evangelism is faithfully communicating an authoritative message from God, one that warns us about our very real need, whether we feel it or not. It is that message that requires a very particular response. And it is that message that, remarkably, converts sinners like you and me by the power of the Holy Spirit.

So the question to ask is not, how do we make the sale? It is, how can we communicate the message? The challenge is not technique, but faithfulness and clarity. Few places better address these matters than 2 Corinthians 4, where Paul describes his own evangelism.

COMMUNICATE PLAINLY

To begin with, we must communicate the gospel message plainly. Paul writes:

> But we have renounced disgraceful, underhanded ways. We refuse to practice cunning or to tamper with God's word, but by the open statement of the truth we would commend ourselves to everyone's conscience in the sight of God. (2 Cor. 4:2)

The gospel has a definite *content*. Successful evangelism for Paul, therefore, is an "open statement of the truth," or as the NIV puts it, "setting forth the truth plainly." Successful evangelism is not getting people to respond. If it were, Paul would have been tempted to resort to "disgraceful, underhanded ways." He might have used "cunning" or "tampered with God's word," trimming and tailoring his preaching to give people what they wanted to hear and so improve his chance at success. But Paul says he has "renounced" all of that.

Also, if successful evangelism is setting forth the truth plainly, it's no good to say, as is sometimes said, "Preach the gospel at all times. If necessary, use words." Apparently both God and Paul believed sharing the good news requires words.

That's not to say there's only one form of words. I find it useful to remember the headings of God, Man, Christ, and Response. But there are other ways to summarize the content. Yet however it's organized, that content must be communicated.

The gospel isn't merely that "God loves you" or "Jesus will give you purpose." It doesn't promise a happy marriage or success at work or successful children. It may help, but it offers no guarantees. The heart of the gospel is that Jesus died and rose again as a substitute for sinners, appeasing God's just wrath and reconciling us to himself.

When we advertise the felt-need benefits of the gospel and neglect the core content of the gospel, we're not doing biblical evangelism but something less. Who doesn't want peace, contentment, and a better family life? It doesn't take the regenerating work of the Holy Spirit to say yes to that offer. George Barna, surveying churchgoing Baby Boomers, observed what felt-needs evangelism offered these consumers.

> For "a one time admission of imperfection and weakness," they received in return "permanent peace with God." The result was that "millions of Boomers who said the prayer, asked for forgiveness and went on with their life, with virtually nothing changed. . . . " [T]hey "saw it as a deal in which they could ex-

ploit God and get what they wanted without giving up anything
of consequence."³

A right doctrine of conversion teaches us to tell people the
good news plainly.

COMMUNICATE HONESTLY

We must communicate honestly, which we do by telling people to count the cost. Paul refers to the cost in the next chapter
of 2 Corinthians: Christ "died for all, that those who live might
no longer live for themselves but for him who for their sake
died and was raised" (2 Cor. 5:15). And Paul learned this from
Jesus: "For whoever would save his life will lose it, but whoever
loses his life for my sake and the gospel's will save it" (Mark
8:35; see also Matt. 16:24).

When we don't ask people to count the cost, but instead
market felt-need benefits, we set them up for failure when suffering and trials come. What happens to their faith in Christ
when young mothers die, kids rebel, or jobs are lost?

Real conversions—conversions characterized by repentance and given by God—bear up under suffering. They treasure Christ and not merely his felt benefits. Did David Brainerd,
who left a promising life in colonial Boston to take the gospel
to the Native Americans, only to die young of tuberculosis,
regret his decision? Did Adoniram Judson, who lost his wife
and children as a missionary in Burma, think he made a mistake? Did William Wilberforce, who sacrificed his chance to be
British prime minister in battling the slave trade, bemoan his
choice? No, they did not. Their testimony was Paul's: "This light

momentary affliction is preparing for us an eternal weight of glory beyond all comparison" (2 Cor. 4:17).

Yet our marketing mind-sets are slow to include the cost of discipleship when evangelizing. We are afraid to tell the whole truth about following Jesus. So we sell the lesser glories. The truth is, Jesus does give his followers a fulfilled life, but it's the fulfillment of knowing that your life is no longer your own and the fulfillment of living for God's glory.

We must proclaim the gospel *honestly*.

COMMUNICATE URGENTLY

Next, biblical evangelism communicates the message with urgency. Consider Paul's own urgency: "Therefore, we are ambassadors for Christ, God making his appeal through us. We implore you on behalf of Christ, be reconciled to God" (2 Cor. 5:20).

The gospel requires a response. Life and death are at stake. Therefore, Paul implores people to "be reconciled." This is not a cool, detached, hip "what do you think?" evangelism. It's earnest, vulnerable, sincere, transparent, urgent.

That's not to say that Paul is rude, pushy, or manipulative. He renounced shameful ways, as we have observed. He worked at removing stumbling blocks (Rom. 14:13; 1 Cor. 8:9). And he was thoughtful about how to approach different groups of people (1 Cor. 9:20–23). So earnestness and urgency do not translate to being offensive or pushy. They do mean he preached "as a dying man to dying men," as the Puritan Richard Baxter famously put it.

How different from so many of us in our postmodern culture! We try to make our message as low-key as possible, as if talking about a lifestyle choice. But doesn't talking about a life-and-death matter as if it's a lifestyle choice communicate to our hearers that we don't actually believe following Christ is a life-and-death matter? The medium is the message, after all.

When proclaiming the gospel, we must urge people to repent and believe today. Life is a vapor, and we don't know when it will end. So the Bible says "Today" is the day to turn if you hear God's voice (Heb. 4:7).

We are ambassadors with a message from a king, not salespeople with consumers to tantalize. We must appeal to people urgently.

COMMUNICATE CONFIDENTLY

Finally, the gospel message is powerful. It doesn't need our help. Therefore, our evangelism can be confident.

Paul knows that not everyone who hears his message becomes a Christian. But does the fault lie with his method or message? No. The problem is the spiritual blindness of unbelievers. Paul writes:

> Even if our gospel is veiled, it is veiled to those who are perishing. In their case the god of this world has blinded the minds of the unbelievers, to keep them from seeing the light of the gospel of the glory of Christ, who is the image of God. (2 Cor. 4:3–4)

Sin and our own corrupt hearts prevent us from seeing the truth. The blindness is willful.

How does Paul get past this blindness? Not with a better method or message. He knows God must do it:

> For what we proclaim is not ourselves, but Jesus Christ as Lord, with ourselves as your servants for Jesus' sake. For God, who said, "Let light shine out of darkness," has shone in our hearts to give the light of the knowledge of the glory of God in the face of Jesus Christ.
>
> But we have this treasure in jars of clay, to show that the surpassing power belongs to God and not to us. (2 Cor. 4:5–7)

The same God who created physical light with a word makes spiritual light shine in the darkness of unbelief with a word. This demonstrates that the "power belongs to God and not to us." Paul proclaims the gospel confidently. He knows God is making his own appeal through Paul and that God's words will create life and light where there is death and darkness.

Why don't we share the gospel more often? For many, I think it's fear and discouragement. We're afraid of being rejected and discouraged that people don't respond. On the other hand, some people are proud of their evangelism and the converts they've made. Yet both the timid and the proud forget that God alone speaks with universe-creating power. We confuse who is responsible for evangelism and who is responsible for the fruit of evangelism. When we do, we err in one of two directions: either we give up or we become pure pragmatists who do whatever it takes to get results. Before long we're engaged in the trickery and manipulation that Paul renounced, and we will create false converts.

Our work is to proclaim a message plainly, honestly, urgently, and confidently. God's work is to save and convert. Recognizing this changes how we measure success. Success for *us* does not depend on results or numbers. It depends on our faithfulness. You and I are not responsible for the results, and so we don't need to pressure or manipulate. We're not trying to close a deal, which—I must say again—creates false converts. Instead, we are free to love, to urge, even to implore with words of warning and words of peace.

That's what evangelism is: God's summons of love to sinners. We're the ambassadors, spokespeople delivering the message. The message is clear: "Be reconciled to God. For our sake he made him to be sin who knew no sin, so that in him we might become the righteousness of God" (2 Cor. 5:20–21). Christian, someone spoke that message to you. With whom can you share it?

7

ASSESS BEFORE
YOU ASSURE

Implications for Ministry

Almost twenty years ago, my family moved to England for graduate school. They were incredibly significant years, but it was so long ago, and so much has happened since, that I can almost find myself wondering, "Did I really do that?" But then I can look at the framed piece of paper hanging on the wall, and there's the proof—a diploma. I really did do that. That framed degree functions a lot like our photographs, proof that something happened that we don't want erased from our memories.

Sometimes we want assurance not because we're afraid we'll forget, but because the matter is too important. Immigration and Customs Enforcement doesn't take my word for it that I'm a citizen. They want proof—a passport. Anyone can say he's a doctor or lawyer, but I like to see the degree hanging on the wall. It's one more piece of evidence that he's legitimate.

Yet some matters are still more important but harder to prove. Am I loved? Do I matter? And for a Christian, there is no more important question than "Do I believe?" Our eternal destiny turns on the answer. Where do we find the proof?

THE QUESTION DEFINED

In chapter 3, I briefly mentioned both the topic of assurance and the "model conversion" of the Thessalonians. I'd like to explore these further, as well as offer practical counsel on how our churches can carefully give wise and biblical assurance.

The topic of assurance is not concerned with the skeptic's question, "Is Christianity true?" It's concerned with the professing Christian's question, "Do *I* believe?" It's not about truth, but about authenticity and credibility.

It's a reasonable question for everyone who claims to be a Christian. Every day we think and do things that call the credibility of our profession into question. We indulge sinful desires. We act like God's angry with us. We proudly do good, thinking it will improve our standing with God. In the face of all this contrary evidence, where do we find assurance that we're believers, and not just deceiving ourselves?

True assurance must ultimately be found by looking at Christ, not by looking for evidences of grace in our lives. Still, the Bible does instruct us to examine the evidence. "Examine yourselves, to see whether you are in the faith" (2 Cor. 13:5). And our churches help us to do this. Done wisely, examination both discomforts the self-deceived and comforts the self-doubting. But do read this chapter together with the next one, which presents the other side of the coin: on the one hand we are to examine ourselves, but on the other hand we are to extend the benefit of the doubt to each other.

Where does a Christian find assurance? Let's explore two possible answers.

IS IT SOMETHING I SAID?

I mentioned in chapter 3 that I once worked with a well-known organization for a big evangelism event. They trained us to lead people in a simple prayer of confession and faith, and then to assure them that they were saved with a dated card as proof.

Christians today look to one main source for assurance that their faith is genuine: words we once said. Did you pray the prayer? Did you confess your sins? Then you're a Christian! That's what I was taught as a child. And I've heard countless others say the same.

The seemingly biblical reason for finding assurance in something we said isn't hard to find. The apostle Paul wrote, "If you confess with your mouth that Jesus is Lord and believe in your heart that God raised him from the dead, you will be saved" (Rom. 10:9). Indeed, our good works don't save us; we're saved through faith, a faith we confess with our lips.

But what is faith? A prayer and a confession? This is where Paul's words to the Thessalonians are so helpful. He says their faith "became an example to all the believers in Macedonia and in Achaia" (1 Thess. 1:7). He continues, "Your faith in God has gone forth everywhere. . . . For they . . . report . . . how you turned to God from idols to serve the living and true God, and to wait for his Son from heaven" (1 Thess. 1:8–10). Paul doesn't point to a prayer they prayed, but to the living trust they display.

Genuine faith has three aspects to it. First, there's *knowledge*. You can't believe something you don't know. Second, there's *agreement*. It's not enough to know the claim that Jesus lived, died as a substitute, and then rose from the dead. You have to agree with it. But third, there is also personal *trust*. It's not enough to know and agree that chairs are for sitting. Faith means sitting down and trusting the chair with your weight. The demons know and agree with the truth about Jesus. But they don't trust Jesus (James 2:17–19).

The Thessalonians didn't just pray a prayer. They actively trusted God in the gospel. Paul says that their faith led them to "turn to God from idols" (call that repentance) "to serve the living and true God, and to wait for his Son from heaven" (call that trust). Theirs was a living hope, not a historical faith.

When we look for assurance in something we once said, two things happen: we assure people that they're saved when they might not be, and we ensure that those who are saved will never find the assurance they need. After all, what if I didn't say the prayer just right or wasn't sufficiently sincere? What if I was just going along with what others expected? What if, what if, what if? I lived with those doubts for years. Far from being assured of my faith, I kept praying again and again, hoping *this time* it would work.

So if assurance isn't found in something we once said, where is it found?

IS IT SOMETHING YOU SEE?

Assuming someone professes Christ, assurance can be found in what others see in you. Paul thanks God for the evidence of grace that demonstrates the Thessalonians are genuine believers. He is confident, and he wants them to be confident too.

We can organize his observations under three categories. First, he points out *evidence of the regenerating work of the Holy Spirit*:

> We give thanks to God always for all of you . . . remembering . . . your work of faith and labor of love and steadfastness of hope in our Lord Jesus Christ. For we know . . . that he has chosen you, because our gospel came to you not only in word, but also in power and in the Holy Spirit and with full conviction. (1 Thess. 1:2–5)

Paul highlights their faith, hope, and love toward God, as well as the power of the Spirit and full conviction. In verse 6 he mentions the joy of the Spirit. To be sure, non-Christians love and act joyfully. But Paul spots something distinct here, a family resemblance with their heavenly Father. It's like the response people give to pictures of my children: "Wow! That's a Lawrence, all right!" In the same way, the Thessalonians' faith, hope, and love demonstrate they've been born of God.

Second, Paul observes their *present, active trust*. He writes:

> And you became imitators of us and of the Lord, for you received the word in much affliction, with the joy of the Holy Spirit. . . . For not only has the word of the Lord sounded forth from you. . . . (1 Thess. 1:6, 8)

They welcomed the message in spite of their afflictions. They shared the gospel. And the reference in verse 3 to "steadfastness of hope" suggests that the opposition the Thessalonians faced has not gone away. This is no historical faith, a prayer they prayed last year. It's something people could see in the present.

Third, Paul points to a *pattern of growth*. They imitate Paul (1 Thess. 1:6). Others make the same "report" (v. 9). Their faith wasn't just a flash in the pan. It continues "stable and steadfast, not shifting from the hope of the gospel" (Col. 1:23).

Assurance is a community project. Paul and others can report to what they've seen, and encourage the Thessalonians accordingly.

When we realize that assurance doesn't just depend on what *I* said but on what *you* see, an amazing thing happens. I stop simply staring at myself, and I invite you to look at me. I in turn look at you. The Christian life and the church change from being about assuring myself to being about assuring you. Suddenly the local church becomes an incredible gift of God to encourage and help us. It's no longer a place to preen and pose, but a place to point out evidences of the Spirit's work in one another's lives—an assurance of faith co-op.

DO I BELIEVE? TELL ME, PLEASE

Here are eight ways we can help each other answer the "Do I believe?" question in the local church.

First, slow the membership process down. It shouldn't be hard to join a church, but unlike the churches I grew up in, you shouldn't be able to join the first Sunday you visit. Put a process in place. That might include a newcomer's lunch, a membership class, and an interview with a pastor. If your church has a plurality of elders, let the elders review and recommend the membership application. If your church is congregational, vote on new members at members' meetings, which tend to happen only four to six times a year. That way, not only will new members have time to get to know the church, but the church will also have time to get to know prospective members and see evidence of the Holy Spirit's work in their lives. (No, I'm not a fan of deliberate probation periods.)

Second, have pastors or elders conduct membership interviews. They are the shepherds whose job is to stand at the gate of the sheep pen. The point of an interview isn't to test people on arcane bits of Bible knowledge or esoteric theology. The point is to take the time to hear a person's story in safety. There's only so much you can learn in the hallway after church. The goal is to understand what's happened in someone's life, how Jesus Christ has changed and is changing them, and to hear their hope in the gospel. Then, when an elder recommends the person's membership to the church, that recommendation is meaningful.

Third, reconsider your practice of baptism and the Lord's Supper. Don't do spontaneous baptisms. Instead, keep baptism and membership connected, the way it was in the New Testament. Other than on the missions frontier, as with the Ethiopian eunuch, the apostles had no category for a baptized Christian who wasn't part of a local church. Devote time in the morning service to hear baptismal testimonies—not of prayers prayed, but of lives changed. When it comes to the Lord's Supper, don't say, "The Tables are open." Take time to explain to each other who should participate in the Supper: baptized members of gospel-preaching local churches. This is what is meant by "fencing the table." The week before, encourage members to examine their hearts and relationships. And even though it's slower, don't do self-serve, drive-thru communion. Serve each other, and then take it together. We don't take the Lord's Supper on our own recognizance, as if the church were just a vending machine. We take it together, saying, "I can see that you believe, and so you belong here." Or in Paul's words: "Because there is one bread, we who are many are one body, for we all partake of the one bread" (1 Cor. 10:17).

Fourth, be especially careful before you assure children of their faith. An untimely or unwarranted assurance can act like a vaccine against true faith. Call children to believe. Teach them and build them up in the faith. When they express faith verbally, celebrate. But remember that the true evidence of faith is trust, and trust needs time and opportunity to demonstrate itself. There's no set age for this. For some, genuine trust will be evident early. For others, it may take longer. Any delay is not about the possibility of a child's regeneration, but about a church's ability to confirm his or her faith with confidence.

Fifth, make membership meaningful. Membership isn't a list of names of people who at some time or another were associated with your church. Membership is a current web of public, accountable relationships. We help each other know that we believe by attending the public services of the church regularly and by building into each other's lives. If you're not present and engaged, building your life into your church, how can you help others know that they believe, and how can they help you?

Sixth, practice church discipline. Church discipline

doesn't mean that you don't like someone or are mad at someone. It doesn't mean that someone made one mistake too many, or that some people are better than others. It doesn't mean someone is going to hell. Church discipline means that you no longer have the evidence you need to assure someone that he believes. That might happen because of consistent, unrepentant sin. But it also might happen because some have cut themselves off from the church, so the church no longer has knowledge of their lives. Regardless of the reason, church discipline is an act of love. All of us are capable of deceiving ourselves about ourselves. Church discipline means that the congregation won't console itself or anyone else falsely by saying, "At least they prayed a prayer when they were a kid." Rather, because of love, the church is not satisfied with historical faith, and won't let you be satisfied with it, either.

Seventh, make the gospel your first recourse in counseling and discipling. The gospel is for Christians because the gospel not only converts us but also produces lasting change in us. Confront sin, lest you risk making people feel more comfortable on their way to hell. But don't confront by saying, "Clean up and try harder; here are some tips and tricks." Instead, call each other to renewed repentance and faith, and so prove to each other that you believe.

Eighth, remember that relationships are as much or more about encouragement than they are accountability. When you see a beloved brother or sister living in a way that's inconsistent with belief, speak gently and in love to correct, exhort, or even rebuke. But even more important, when you see faith, hope, and love, be quick to point that out. Sometimes it is hard to assure ourselves. Our sins are always in front of us, clouding our view. Our perspective is so often dominated by the pressing sin and the failure of the moment. That's when we need someone else to look at us, and to point out the longer-term growth, the present trust, and the fruit of the Spirit that we often cannot see in ourselves.

Do I believe? Do you? So many Christians are trying to live the Christian life on their own. So many churches practice a thin, consumer-Christianity that leaves you alone, struggling to answer the question. Praise God for healthy local churches, because none of us can do this on our own. I need to know if I believe, or if I'm just fooling myself. And so do you. That means we need the church.

8

CHARITABLE, NOT CHARY

The Danger of an Overly Pure Church

Two famous poets reflect on the nature of human inter-action:

> "No man is an island, entire of itself; every man is a piece of the continent, a part of the main." John Donne (1624)

> "I am a rock, I am an island, And a rock feels no pain, and an island never cries." Paul Simon (1965)

In between those two poets lies one of the great emotional tensions of our lives. We were made for community. We cannot live alone. And yet, to enter into community is to risk the profound pain of rejection and exclusion. Perhaps it's easier to be an island after all.

This tension starts early, at school or on the sports team. It intensifies in college. It plays itself out at work, which turns out to be more like high school, with its in-groups and out-groups, than we'd like to admit. It seems we never outgrow the longing or the question: Do I belong?

Then there's church. Do I belong here? In the gospel, we learn that God accepts us through Jesus Christ. But what about God's people? Do they accept me?

THE QUESTION DEFINED

Many Christians walk into a church and wonder, "Do I fit in here?" Knowing this, many churches structure themselves around something that will make a target audience feel at home, things like ethnicity, education, socioeconomics, age, or culture, just to name a few.

There's much to commend for being welcoming and accessible, but there's a problem with this approach. For one thing, no one ever seems to target the ugly, the unpopular, and the out-of-touch. Also, what of James's warnings against favoritism (James 2:1–5)? Do they not apply if the goal is church growth and evangelism?

Non-Christians are not asking, "Do I fit in?" They have plenty of places to go where they fit in. Rather, many non-Christians are intrigued by the idea of genuine community. They, too, want feelings of belonging. In fact, there's a whole philosophy of ministry that encourages pastors to attract non-Christians by letting them belong before they believe. Once they find meaningful community in your church, the thinking goes, they're more likely to become believers.

This approach is popular today, but in fact there is no such thing as "belonging before believing." To belong to God's people means that you have been rescued from the kingdom of darkness and brought into the kingdom of light through faith in Jesus Christ (Col. 1:12–13). It's because we believe that we belong, and never the other way around.

"Do I belong?" isn't the question of the consumer or the seeker. It's the question of the doubter. In the previous chapter we saw that the church is a gift from God to assure us that we are genuine believers. But where do we set the bar? Let's consider two possible answers.

I BELONG BECAUSE OF MY HOLINESS

In the last chapter, we emphasized the role of external evidence for giving assurance to one another. But as soon as we adopt the Bible's teaching that we should accept only the genuinely converted into church membership, thereby assuring them of their faith, we are immediately in danger of falling off the other side of the horse. We know we should look for a love of God's truth, a turning away from sin, and a willingness to obey God. But how much moral, personal, and doctrinal purity is enough; how little is too little? It is all too easy to become chary, that is, suspiciously reluctant, of accepting anyone who doesn't measure up to our standards, either personally or corporately.

This is what non-Christians fear about us: that we think we're better; that belonging to a church means being a good person whose life, politics, and clothing are "right."

When we become chary of accepting others based on our measure of holiness, we have become Pharisees. It's the mistake of fundamentalism, and it's a danger that all conservative, theologically minded churches face. Jesus never condemned the Pharisees for their holiness. What he condemned them for was reducing holiness to an outward list of do's and don'ts that they could manage, and then judging everyone else by their own measure.

If holiness—however you define it—is how you know you belong, how do you decide as a church if someone belongs? How holy is holy enough?

I BELONG BECAUSE OF MY HOPE

In the first chapter of 1 Corinthians, Paul points us to a better answer to our question.

> I give thanks to my God always for you because of the grace of God that was given you in Christ Jesus, that in every way you were enriched in him in all speech and all knowledge—even as the testimony about Christ was confirmed among you—so that you are not lacking in any gift, as you wait for the revealing of our Lord Jesus Christ, who will sustain you to the end, guiltless in the day of our Lord Jesus Christ. (1 Cor. 1:4–8)

Consider Paul's praise. He thanks God for the grace they've received. He is glad that they are enriched in speech and knowledge. He affirms they possess Christ's testimony. He says they don't lack any gift, as they patiently await the Lord's return. These first few verses sound almost as positive and encouraging as the opening to 1 Thessalonians that we considered in the last chapter.

That quickly changes, however. These are some of the last positive things Paul will say about the Corinthians for the rest of the letter. At the start of chapter 3, he calls them "infants," "of the flesh," and immature, "not yet ready for solid food" (vv. 1–3). Yet these opening lines are crucial because they let us see Paul's charity toward the Corinthians. They don't belong because they're mature and perfect in holiness. They belong because their hope is in Jesus Christ, and that hope is reorienting their lives.

What happens when we are charitable rather than chary? Using the rest of 1 Corinthians, I want to point out five surprising groups of people who belong in our churches because their hope is in Jesus Christ.

The Immature

Paul calls the Corinthian Christians "infants in Christ" in chapter 3. Their *doctrine* is not what it should be. From their understanding of the nature and growth of the church (chap. 3), to their theology of worship (chap. 14), to the future resurrection (chap. 15), they have a lot to learn. And their ignorance is causing trouble and division in the church. Fights are breaking out! But it's not just the church's doctrine. Their understanding of the Christian *life* is immature. They're all mixed up on whether you can eat food sacrificed to idols (chap. 8), and they have terrible ideas about marriage and singleness (chap. 7). And yet, for all this immaturity, Paul calls them "brothers" and affirms they are "in Christ."

For some of our churches, this is an issue we need to grapple with. Our churches should be concerned with right living and right doctrine. But whether we have come out of more liberal denominations, or were founded in an effort to recover biblical Christianity, can we be charitable toward those who

113

have not yet arrived to the measure of growth that we have? Is there room in our conservative churches for someone to belong who is less mature?

The Imperfect

Another group that belongs is the imperfect. That's not Paul's language; it's Eleazer Savage's. He was a Northern Baptist pastor in Connecticut in the early 1800s, and it's how he describes those Christians who must be borne with. In that category, he includes the irritable, the loquacious, the obtrusive, the shirker, and the petty, among others.[1] These could fall under the category of immature, but the difference is that some of these character faults might never change in a person, no matter how mature they become in other ways. We see these people in 1 Corinthians 1 and 3 taking sides in petty quarrels and silly factions. We see them in chapter 14 unwilling to stop talking and let someone else have a word. We see them in chapter 12 proudly promoting their own gifts. And yet, while Paul has no praise for these character faults, he says to them, "You are the body of Christ and individually members of it" (12:27). We each have character flaws that make us limp, and we may limp our whole lives. We have to bear with one another's limps, because if your hope is in Christ, you belong.

The Weak

It's clear that though the Corinthians have turned to Christ, they continue to struggle with sin, and not just garden-variety sin. Paul confronts sexual immorality (chap. 6), unbiblical divorce (chap. 7), and drunkenness (chap. 11). Paul doesn't wink and nod at such sin. He doesn't sweep it under the carpet. At one point he tells the Corinthians, "Flee from sexual immorality" (6:18). Yet in the very same breath he affirms their faith by asking, "Or do you not know that your body is a temple of the Holy Spirit within you, whom you have from God?" (6:19). In other words, Paul knows that genuine Christians are weak in the flesh and struggle with sin. But he extends them charity because their struggle is evidence of their hope.

Years ago I worked with a young man who struggled with serious sexual immorality, including the use of prostitutes. It was heartbreaking. There were moments when the elders of the church seriously considered church discipline. What held us back was that he was genuinely struggling. Every time it happened, he came to us to confess, and he invited us further into his life. It would have been easy for him to hide and lie to us, but he didn't. So the church walked with this weak, struggling brother. We didn't say, "You don't belong." We said, "We're going to walk with you in your weakness and in your struggle."

Hypocrites who hide and lie are not hoping in Christ, even though outwardly they look fine. It's the open, honest struggle that demonstrates true hope in Christ.

The Wounded

It's not just that we struggle with sin. We have been sinned against, and we respond sinfully. In our pain we lash out to prevent further hurt. We numb the pain with other sins, rather than the balm of the gospel. Perhaps that is part of what's happening in 1 Corinthians 6. Paul rebukes the Corinthians because "brother goes to law against brother, and that before unbelievers" (v. 6). You know how this works: the best defense is a good offense, so when someone sues you, you countersue.

But Paul replies, "Why not rather suffer wrong? Why not rather be defrauded?" (1 Cor. 6:7). He calls the Corinthians to respond to insult with grace, to respond to attack with forgiveness and love. This doesn't mean we should submit to abuse. It does mean that our response to being sinned against is to be conditioned by the gospel, rather than by our pain. But notice once again, Paul still calls them "brothers."

The Scandalous

There's one category that Paul says does not belong in the church, and to whom he does not extend charity. That's the wicked, or the unrepentant. It's not that Paul doesn't love even these, but it's tough love they should receive. So in 1 Corinthians 5, he calls the church to "purge the evil person from among you" (v. 13). Due to the man's significant and unrepentant sin, the church can no longer affirm that the man is a brother.

Yet then something amazing happens. In 2 Corinthians 2, Paul tells the church, "This punishment by the majority is enough, so you should rather turn to forgive and comfort him, or he may be overwhelmed by excessive sorrow" (2 Cor. 2:6–7). Many believe this is the same man from 1 Corinthians 5. He appears to have repented in sorrow. So Paul tells the church to take him back in, to forgive and comfort him with the knowledge that he belongs. There is no sin so scandalous, no personal history so distasteful, that it cannot be forgiven by the grace of Jesus Christ for those who repent and put their hope in him. If Christ does not reject the repentant murderer, or homosexual, or child abuser, can we?

The truth is, all our names are somewhere in this list. Are you immature in your doctrine or your life? Are there character flaws that others must bear with? Do you struggle with sin, and having been sinned against? Do you bring a history of sin that is shameful and scandalous? Regardless of how many categories you find yourself in, if your hope is in Christ, you belong in his church.

Hope in Christ demonstrates itself in a trajectory of growth, not by having already arrived. It's seen in a willingness to be taught, not in already knowing everything. It struggles against sin; it's not at ease in Zion (Amos 6:1). It limps with the wounds of battle, but limping on it goes. And it holds on to the trustworthy saying "that Christ Jesus came into the world to save sinners, of whom I am the foremost" (1 Tim. 1:15). No shame is so great that it cannot be comprehended by the shame of the cross of Christ, and there be redeemed to everlasting glory.

Paul called the Corinthians infants, immature, and unspiritual. He did not reject them for that, but neither did he want them to stay there. He called them to grow up, and to do so in the community of the church, which is the school of faith, not the hall of fame of faith. To change the image, if the church is God's vineyard, we're not finally fruit inspectors, but gardeners, working with each other to see the fruit of faith formed.

What does that look like? At my own church, it looks like

this: you confess the gospel through baptism; you articulate your hope in the gospel; you agree with our basic statement of faith and government; and you testify to your desire to grow in your hope in Christ. If this is you, you can belong.

Years ago I interviewed a young engaged couple for membership. She had grown up in the church and her story and her answers were textbook perfect. He came out of a life of addiction and immorality, and his answers were earnest at best. Still, coming out of the interview, he had the spark of spiritual life about him, and she did not. We took them both into membership. It was a long engagement. I did their premarital counseling. By the end I pulled him aside and privately urged him not to get married. She was a member in good standing in our church, but I was more convinced than ever that she wasn't alive spiritually, but dead in her sins. The marriage went ahead, and for years, the church walked with them through what proved to be a difficult marriage. He was growing as a Christian, and she was not. They eventually moved away, where their marriage ended in heartbreak and divorce, as she left him.

Did we make a mistake years earlier by admitting her to membership? No, we did not. For all my intuitions, I cannot see the heart, and neither can you. In charity we said, "You belong." In charity, we walked with her, bearing with her and gently calling her to the life of faith. Had I to do it all over again, I would make the same decision. The church is not for those who have arrived in heaven, but for those whose hopes are oriented there. Some prove false in their hope. But others, even those who come weak and wounded, sick and sore, do not prove false. It is for people like us that Christ died and built a church, that together we might become what Paul describes at the very end of his letter to the Corinthians: "firm in the faith, men and women of courage, strong, doing everything in charity," which is just an old-fashioned word for love.[2]

CONCLUSION

When I moved from the East Coast of America to the West Coast, I entered the ranks of frustrated voters. By the time the presidential elections reach the West Coast every Election Day, which includes the most populous state in the nation, the East Coast and Midwest have made the outcome of the election clear. And if the outcome is already determined, do our votes even matter?

The same question might be asked about our doctrine of conversion in the life of the church. If conversion is God's work, and he's sovereign over salvation, does it really matter how we work out the doctrine of conversion in our life together? If there's nothing we can do to prevent his elect, chosen people from being saved, does it really matter how we practice evangelism or give assurance? If the outcome is assured, aren't we sort of like the West Coast on election night?

Surveying the landscape of conservative, Reformed evangelical churches in America today, it appears our doctrine doesn't matter. Pragmatism, rather than theology, seems to be our guide in everything from evangelism to worship to membership (or lack thereof). We pursue whatever seems to work, even if that practice contradicts what we say about how a person crosses from death into life.

But in fact our doctrine of conversion does matter. In the first century, Peter wrote to churches scattered through modern Turkey who were under pressure because they were out of step with the surrounding culture, a situation not unlike our own. Tempted toward pragmatic accommodation, Peter writes to encourage them to remain faithful. After discussing their salvation and life together, Peter draws this conclusion:

> But you are a chosen race, a royal priesthood, a holy nation, a people for his own possession, that you may proclaim the excellencies of him who called you out of darkness into his marvelous light. Once you were not a people, but now you are God's people; once you had not received mercy, but now you have received mercy.
>
> Beloved, I urge you as sojourners and exiles to abstain from the passions of the flesh, which wage war against your soul. Keep your conduct among the Gentiles honorable, so that when they speak against you as evildoers, they may see your good deeds and glorify God on the day of visitation. (1 Pet. 2:9–12)

In this passage, our theology of conversion matters for at least three reasons.

IT MATTERS FOR GOD

Peter begins by pointing out what God has done. God chose us. God possesses us. God made us a people. God gave us mercy. God called us out of darkness into his marvelous light. This is not like me calling my kids to dinner, and certainly not like calling them to do their chores. Maybe they respond, maybe they don't. My call is a request, an invitation that can be accepted or not. God's call is a summons that accomplishes what he intends.

God accomplished our salvation through the death and resurrection of Christ, and he sovereignly applies that salvation to us through his sovereign saving call. He gives us ears to hear the call. He gives us a new heart to respond to the call. He gives us the twin graces of repentance and faith to grasp hold of the salvation extended in the call.

So why exactly does our theology of conversion matter? Peter answers, "That you may proclaim the excellencies of him who called you." It matters to God. We naturally read that *you* as singular. But it's not. It's plural in the original language. Peter is writing to churches, not individuals. To understand Peter we need to translate this verse into American Southern: so that y'all may proclaim the excellencies of him who called y'all.

God wants you personally to praise him for his salvation, but Jesus didn't die just for you, he died for his people, and God wants to hear from his people. You might shout for joy by yourself in your living room watching your favorite team win a game on television. But the noise is quite a bit louder in the arena where the game is played. God's purpose is to hear from the whole arena.

That will ultimately happen on the last day, but we get previews of it in the local church. It matters who gathers each Sunday to sing God's praises. People might like the friendships or benefit from the programs. But they can do that without being born again. If God is going to be truly praised, the local church needs people who have actually experienced God's rescue.

Local church worship isn't an intellectual exercise. It's praise for what God has actually done in our lives. This is why there can be no such thing as "belonging before believing." There can be attending or involvement before believing. But there can be no belonging, because God's purpose for belonging is praising, and we cannot praise him for something we have not experienced.

I recently talked to a pastor whose church hired a consultant to help them boost their numbers. The consultant told them they got church wrong. Church isn't for believers, they were told, it's for unbelievers. So they needed to change their practice to make church more attractive to unbelievers, and that meant more entertaining. At one level the consultant was right. If the goal is a bigger crowd, entertainment works. But that's not God's goal for the church. He wants the praise of his people, people who know they have received mercy.

The difference between church as a crowd and church as a gathering of believers is the difference between those who want entertainment and those who love God and switched their allegiance to him. It's the difference between a consumer of religious experiences and a producer of praise to the glories of Christ crucified.

Our theology of conversion matters, because it reorients our understanding of the purpose of our assembly and the meaning of our membership. If our churches aren't filled with believers, then God is robbed of the praise he desires and deserves.

IT MATTERS FOR US

Second, our doctrine of conversion matters to us. Peter reminds us we are "sojourners and exiles" and to keep our distance from the sinful desires that "wage war against" our souls.

For a Christian, the guilt of sin is removed. And the power of sin is broken. But the presence of sin remains, and this is not a trivial matter. Sin means to murder us. As one Puritan observed, "Be killing sin, or it will be killing you."[1] Once again this is where our theology of conversion in the life of the church matters. The battle against sin gives us assurance that we really believe, and the fact that we are not alone in the battle makes all the difference. We cannot help each other in this battle if we don't know we're in the battle or are not engaged in the fight.

We need each other in the fight. We need fellow church members who understand how hard the fight is, who know how to help and encourage us, who understand that spurring one another on in the faith is a life-and-death matter over which the day of judgment looms (Heb. 10:25). How discouraging and confusing to battle against sin, only to look to our right or left and see fellow church members, either standing by the side or even consorting with the enemy!

I once knew a Christian leader who was a gifted counselor. People would come with their problems—broken marriages, family conflict, anxiety and depression—and all of them would walk away genuinely helped by his wisdom and counsel. All, that is, except one group: young men dealing with homosexuality. When they came to his office, he taught them to be discreet about their sexual orientation, and where to meet up safely with other young men for liaisons. It turned out this leader also experienced same-sex attraction, but he lost interest in the battle. He eventually left the faith altogether. And how many young men did he dissuade from battling against the sin that wars against the soul?

A college friend of mine found her marriage breaking up, as her husband left her for another woman. She went to her church leaders for help, but they told her there was nothing they could do. Soon her evangelical church welcomed her former husband and his new wife into the church. And she was left in a dark night of the soul that took years to recover from. How many spouses tempted by adultery in that church were helped in their battle against the sin that wars against the soul?

Our theology of conversion matters in our churches' discipleship, gospel counsel, and even church discipline, because the presence of sin remains, and we are the walking wounded. We need each other's help in churches filled with people who will battle with us.

IT MATTERS FOR THE WORLD

Third, our doctrine of conversion matters for the world's sake. By looking at our churches, the world gains assurance that there is a God and that the hope of change exists. Peter knows that when the world sees our "honorable" conduct and "good deeds," they might "speak against" us, but they will also "glorify God."

Peter says this will happen on "the day of visitation." It's quite possible this phrase refers to the day of judgment. But I don't think that's what Peter has in mind. Throughout Scripture, the day of God's visitation is the day of salvation, and we glorify God by believing him.[2]

If the world looks at the church and sees only itself with a lot of religious speech tacked on, how can they have confidence that there is a God who gives hope for something different? If they see the church posturing and pretending, they'll regard it as a lie. But if they see lives that are genuinely changed and changing, some, Peter teaches, will glorify God on that day by becoming Christians.

Some years ago, an older gentleman began visiting the church to which I belonged. It was a church full of young people, and so quite naturally he stayed on the edge of the community. But he didn't go away. He observed. He listened. He got to know many of us. And the day came when he put his faith in Christ. In his baptismal testimony he explained what had happened. It turns out he was a psychiatrist and university professor. All of his training had taught him that what he was seeing in that church wasn't possible: genuine community that crossed natural barriers; real change that wasn't just therapeutic adjustment; self-sacrificing love for others that was not transactional. He realized that the only thing that could explain what he was seeing was that God was real and the gospel of Jesus Christ was true.

The local church is God's evangelism plan for the world. The local church is the world's assurance that Jesus got up from the dead. Our genuinely converted lives, our authentically Christian community, our dependence upon grace rather than technique, is God's apologetic to unbelief. This is why both our theology of conversion and the practice that flows from it matter for the world. If the world doesn't see this truth in us, then where will they see it?

God chooses and God saves. Conversion is his work. And yet he uses means to accomplish his predetermined ends. One of those means is the local church. We give witness to the gospel with our words. Then we make those words plausible with our lives. For God, for ourselves, and for the world, it matters that we get this doctrine right, and that we work it out faithfully in the life of the church.

NOTES

Chapter 1: New, Not Nice

1. For both an example and the philosophy that drives this program, visit these two pages on the World Weavers website: http://www.worldweavers.com/cambodia-spiritual-adventure and http://www.worldweavers.com/about-us.

Chapter 2: Saved, Not Sincere

1. Fanny Crosby, "To God Be the Glory," 1875.

2. Bruce Waltke, *The Book of Proverbs: Chapters 1–15*, New International Commentary on the Old Testament (Grand Rapids, MI: Eerdmans, 2004), 211.

3. Charles Wesley, "And Can It Be That I Should Gain," 1738.

Chapter 3: Disciples, Not Decisions

1. Dietrich Bonhoeffer, *The Cost of Discipleship*, rev. ed. (New York: MacMillan, 1963), 99.

2. Charles H. Spurgeon, "The Metropolitan Tabernacle Pulpit," in *Spurgeon Sermon Collection*, Accordance electronic ed., 2 vols. (Altamonte Springs, FL: OakTree Software, 2012), paragraph 62026.

3. Gordon T. Smith, *Transforming Conversion: Rethinking the Language and Contours of Christian Initiation* (Grand Rapids, MI: Baker Academic, 2010), 148.

4. John Piper, "Hope in Eternal Purity," Desiring God website, November 4, 2015, http://www.desiringgod.org/interviews/hope-in -eternal-purity-aim-at-daily-purity.

Chapter 4: Holy, Not Healed

1. Oprah Winfrey, "The O Interview: Oprah Talks to Phil Donahue," *O, The Oprah Magazine*, September 2002, 214.

2. Kevin DeYoung, *The Hole in Our Holiness: Filling the Gap between Gospel Passion and the Pursuit of Godliness* (Wheaton, IL: Crossway, 2012), 18.

Chapter 6: Summon, Don't Sell

1. Lloyd Wendt, *Give the Lady What She Wants! The Story of Marshall Field & Company* (New York: Rand McNally, 1952), 223.

2. Rick Warren, *The Purpose Driven Church* (Grand Rapids, MI: Zondervan, 1995), 219.

3. Quoted in David Wells, *Above All Earthly Pow'rs: Christ in a Post-Modern World* (Grand Rapids, MI: Eerdmans, 2005), 302.

Chapter 8: Charitable, Not Chary

1. Eleazar Savage, *Manual of Church Discipline* (1863), in Mark E. Dever, ed., *Polity: Biblical Arguments on How to Conduct Church Life* (Washington, DC: Center for Church Reform, 2001), 487.

2. 1 Corinthians 16:13–14, author's translation.

Conclusion

1. John Owen, *Of the Mortification of Sin in Believers; the Necessity, Nature, and Means of it: with a Resolution of Sundry Cases of Conscience thereunto belonging*, in *The Works of John Owen*, ed. William H. Goold, vol. 6 (Edinburgh: Banner of Truth Trust, 1967), 9.

2. Thomas R. Schreiner, *1, 2 Peter, Jude*, The New American Commentary, vol. 37 (Nashville, TN: Broadman & Holman, 2003), 124.

GENERAL INDEX

SCRIPTURE INDEX

9Marks

Building Healthy Churches

9Marks exists to equip church leaders with a biblical vision and practical resources for displaying God's glory to the nations through healthy churches.

To that end, we want to see churches characterized by these nine marks of health:

1. Expositional Preaching
2. Gospel Doctrine
3. A Biblical Understanding of Conversion and Evangelism
4. Biblical Church Membership
5. Biblical Church Discipline
6. A Biblical Concern for Discipleship and Growth
7. Biblical Church Leadership
8. A Biblical Understanding of the Practice of Prayer
9. A Biblical Understanding and Practice of Missions

Find all our Crossway titles and other resources at 9Marks.org.

9MARKS: BUILDING HEALTHY CHURCHES SERIES

Based on Mark Dever's best-selling book *Nine Marks of a Healthy Church*, each book in this series helps readers grasp basic biblical commands regarding the local church.

TITLES INCLUDE:

Biblical Theology	Corporate Worship	The Gospel
Church Discipline	Deacons	Missions
Church Elders	Discipling	Prayer
Church Membership	Evangelism	Sound Doctrine
Conversion	Expositional Preaching	

For more information, visit crossway.org.
For translated versions of these and other 9Marks books, visit 9Marks.org/bookstore/translations.